INTRODUCTION

When the British occupied the Faroe Islands during the Second World War, they called this beguiling place 'the land of maybe'. As in, 'maybe the weather will change, maybe it won't. Maybe the boat will come, maybe it won't.'

For the Faroese, the phrase means more than just 'maybe'. It is a state of mind and a context that I drew upon when I perused the start lists for the final of the men's 1500 metres freestyle at the 2010 European Swimming Championships in Budapest.

Covering the sport for the first time for the *Daily Telegraph*, with no Brits in action, I breathed a sigh of relief. It was a chance to sit back and take in the atmosphere at the wonderful Alfred Hajos swimming complex on Margaret Island.

Hungarians love their water, preferably natural and hot. There are centuries-old baths spread across the capital, while the raft of sprawling aqua parks do a roaring trade throughout the summer.

This particular 1500m final had no local swimmers, so it would be a quiet fifteen minutes, without vuvuzelas at least, for the sport's longest discipline in a long course 50m pool.

Halfway through the race, I looked down the start list to pick out the leader, a few lengths or so ahead of the pack. I found the name: Pal Joensen. Next to his start lane was his country: FAR.

The Faroe Islands? Surely not. Most sport fans in Britain only knew the country, wherever it was, for the habitual beatings inflicted on its football team in European or World Cup qualifiers. A 5-0 defeat to the Republic of Ireland here, a 6-0 loss to Germany there.

Except that this Faroe Islander was faring rather well. Maybe the swimmer from the land of maybe would win.

It was a thrilling denouement. For whatever reason – and I'm now extremely glad I did this – I raced down to the mixed zone (the walk through where reporters catch out-of-breath swimmers) to try and grab a few words with this gallant islander.

Joensen seemed surprised to be stopped and I was the only journalist wanting to speak to him, bar a prying microphone from the Championship media team. Despite leading at the turn but eventually ending up with second place, he seemed to want to be next to a microphone. Others would have wanted to be anywhere but.

British journalist Rod Gilmour has been described by *The Guardian* as a 'minor sport tub-thumper'. He co-authored James Willstrop's *Shot and a Ghost: A Year in the Brutal World of Professional Squash*, which was nominated for the William Hill Sports Book of the Year award, the first self-published book to be nominated. He has covered Olympic sports for the *Daily Telegraph* since 2008.

THE
PAL EFFECT

A Faroe Islander's Quest for
Swimming Glory

ROD GILMOUR

Chequered Flag
PUBLISHING

First published in the UK by Chequered Flag Publishing
PO Box 4669, Sheffield, S6 9ET
www.chequeredflagpublishing.co.uk

A CIP record for this book is available from the British Library

Printed in the EU by Print Group Sp. z o.o.

Picture acknowledgements
Cover: Benjamin Rasmussen/Tryggingarfelagið Føroyar
p 22: Visit Faroe Islands
All other images courtesy Rokur i Jakupsstovu

ISBN 9780993215223

To Dad, who loved his early morning swimming.

CONTENTS

Introduction   1

1   These Magnificent Islands   9
2   Glorious Defeats   23
3   Seeds of Success   39
4   Road to London   51
5   The Horrible Flop   67
6   The Pal Effect   83
7   The Faroes and the Worlds   101
8   From Budapest to Berlin   121
9   Pal's Pool   141

The Extra Lengths:
Tackling the 1500 metres   157
Rod Gilmour

Pal is a living, breathing Faroese hero   163
Rokur i Jakupsstovu, President of Faroe Islands Swimming Federation

We don't tend to brag in the Faroes   170
Malan Joensen, wife of Pal Joensen

Records and Medals   175

Acknowledgements   181

My country where the Atlantic current head strong goes
On the globe is butter dot
Winter sang you a song of might
And summer a gentle song of love
When in foreign lands keep in mind your little home
In sun as well as dressed in snow
The northern lights brightly glow but quickly change
Like tender young dreams on a summer's night

Extracts taken from Faroese poet Poul F Joensen (1898-1970), a distant relative of Pal Joensen.

'I think that's the first international medal in any sport for my country, but in swimming that's a fact,' were his first words to me.

He went on to reveal that his success in recent years had led the Faroese Sportsperson of the Year award to be scrapped after he had won the New Years' Eve gong so often. Bless those footballers.

Further, he added that he could only train in a 25m pool – it was originally 12.5m – back on his home island of Suduroy, the most southerly of the Faroes' eighteen. My eyes opened wider. Joensen was an 800m and 1500m swimmer after all, so his Budapest bounty was certainly some feat.

Asked what welcome he might receive on his return, Joensen hinted that it would be a 'big evening'. It should be a national holiday, I wrote at the end of an article I sent in for the *Telegraph*.

No one really remembers the minor medals, but this felt like pure gold.

When I got back to the UK, I began researching Pal's career. Ultimately, it was a YouTube clip from a local documentary maker that heralded the start of a five-year project on this affable islander's rise, from training in a small pool to racing on the big stage.

I urge you to watch it to get an early sense of this story. For this you can go to the video section at this book's companion website, www.thepaleffect.tumblr.com, and watch the clip capturing the emotion of Joensen's return to the islands after winning three golds at the 2008 European Junior Championships.

The water cannons over the plane; the tears rolling down those young Faroese cheeks; the ride on the back of a truck as he travels round the island; the fish factory workers, in white overalls, who congregate outside their workplace and wave to their new hero; what looks like the Suduroy branch of the Hells Angels following the vehicle's every move.

The clip struck an immediate chord, if only for the fact that it simply wouldn't happen in the UK. Open-top bus parades and gold post boxes after Olympic gold, yes, but nothing like this for a silver medal.

I kept up with Pal's career as the London 2012 Olympics loomed, though the Games were an unmitigated disaster for him. Joensen found the pressure and emotion too much – for reasons which will be outlined in these pages.

Undeterred, less than a year later I travelled out to the Faroes. A place of curious and mysterious beauty, with a population of around 49,000, I met the Prime Minister, travelled by boat to Joensen's home island, attended the National Championships and refrained from buying a knitted sweater made famous by *The Killing*.

I then charted Joensen's campaigns at both the Barcelona World Championships in 2013 and the 2014 European Championships in Berlin. All the while, I learnt more about Faroese swimming from passionate and indefatigable flagbearers, Rokur i Jakupsstovu and Jon Hestoy, the former taking over from the latter as Faroese Swimming Federation president in 2014.

At the same time, I questioned when a suitable ending for a book might occur. Mulling over whether to wait for the dream of an Olympic medal at Rio 2016 and the greatest moment ever in Faroese history, I recalled something that Rokur had told me on a night out in the capital, Torshavn.

We were talking about his upbringing on the island and the stories that he had been fed as a child. All of them, he said, were about glorious, mythological failures.

Oh well, there's always next time: the age-old mantra of the Faroese, which included, in today's sporting context, the results of the country's national football team.

Then along came Joensen. The Pal Effect was born; his name a positive symbol for schools and businesses in a society where success really was achievable.

I discovered that this wasn't just a story of one man's rise from a small pool to elite swimmer. After all, plenty of athletes have been forced to train in equally tough conditions.

The simplicity and remoteness of his upbringing in Suduroy left Pal and his fellow club teammates with few distractions other than to focus on swimming, as well as a coach who just happened to be rather good at his job.

As the book neared completion, we had several chats over how the book would be conveyed. 'What is it that makes you decide something?' Pal said.

He was referring to economical and sociological values. The sociologist perspective (the mind set of human behaviour and its connection to society) was that you follow the norms and values of your surroundings, while the economist's perspective was that individuals made their decisions based on calculating what benefits you get and at what cost.

While he wasn't saying that everyone should step out of their normal surroundings, what he hoped *The Pal Effect* would reflect was that 'pursuing one's desire and investing a lot of time and energy to do something extraordinary, will become normal'.

'I haven't followed anyone in my pursuit of my goals,' he told me late into the project. 'I didn't do as everyone else. Instead I invested a lot of my time in something I was counting on might benefit my future.'

As he has done this, so he has lifted a tiny nation in the middle of the North Atlantic. And if not a whole nation, then his home village, whose intuitive Mayor conceived, in 2010, a project of truly 'crazy' proportions. They built Pal's Pool.

1

THESE MAGNIFICENT ISLANDS

And now the Shipping Forecast…
Faeroes
Wind: south-westerly 3, increasing 4 or 5, occasionally 6
in north-west later.
Sea state: moderate, occasionally rough at first.
Weather: occasional rain.
Visibility: moderate or good.

Those wonderfully evocative names relayed daily on the BBC Shipping Forecast – Dogger, Viking, Bailey, Rockall, to name but a few – include one location which proves it is closer to mainland Britain than many people think.

Though the corporation's spelling, Faeroes, suggests that these lands are far away from the British Isles, the Faroe Islands are not indeed in Portugal, Egypt (Pharoahs, perhaps?) or Polynesia as some believe.

The Faroe Islands are a mountainous archipelago of eighteen islands, lying north of Scotland – the Shetland Islands are 370 kilometres south-east of the Faroes' capital, Torshavn – and halfway between Norway and Iceland.

In 1673, Lucas Jacobsen Debes presented his study *Faeroe and Faeroa Reserata*, the first printed work about the Faroe Islands and the first attempt to bring the islands out from obscurity.

Unknown to the ancient Greeks and Romans, the islands' first discoverers were daring Norsemen in the ninth century – though the first settlers were probably Irish monks back in the seventh century – who sailed the seas for new shores to plunder.

Wild, remote and beautiful, the islands run at their own pace and offer isolation and recuperation in abundance, bustling with atmosphere, wildlife, pastures… and no trees anywhere. Unsurprisingly, the name is derived from the word *faar*, or *foer*, a sheep. There are supposedly 20,000 more sheep than people living in the Faroes, despite recent human population growth. The current population of around 49,000 has increased from 15,000 at the turn of 1900.

Flying in past mightily jagged cliffs and pastures, then driving the road from Vagar, where the airport is situated, is simply stunning. Bulging with waterfalls at every turn, the road hugs the fjords most of the way into the capital, barring the plethora of tunnels which makes the passage both easier and shorter.

Travel into Torshavn port by ferry and you are immediately hit by the rocky promontory of Tinganes, home of the Faroese parliament for over a thousand years. It must rank as one of the more striking governmental buildings anywhere in the world.

The area is home to some of the oldest homes in the city, dating back to the fourteenth century. Tinganes stands out with its red-painted coating and grass-turfed roofs. Behind these buildings, up winding inclines, are smaller houses with more grass roofs to provide insulation and sound proofing. Occasionally you see men mowing the roofs, or sheep grazing.

The weather is utterly changeable. It can be short-sleeve order one moment, yellow fishing jackets the next. In summer months, it is dark for just a few hours. In winter, there is a short period in the day when the light shines, but most people still feel tired.

The eighteen islands, separated by fjords and sounds, are well-serviced, but they remain remote. Each has their own voice and the people are seen to have their own character. Life is slow here. Just as it should be.

The mountains on many of the islands dominate the landscape, the bays pierce more deeply into the land. And with more than 1,100 kilometres of coastline, you are never more than five kilometres away from the sea.

Most of the islands rise from the ocean surrounded by walls of lofty rocks. The cliffs are so perpendicular that boats used to be let down by ropes while sailors clambered up the sides from holes cut into the rocks. The Faroes resemble Elba, except there is no prison on any of the islands. There are three traffic lights though.

The water is cold and usually jags deep within metres, none more so than on Suduroy. With its interjectory fjords, Suduroy, forty-four square miles in size, is the Faroes' most southerly island.

The island's shape and character is perhaps best summed up by the *Historical and Descriptive Account of Iceland, Greenland and the Faroe Islands*, printed by an Edinburgh publisher in 1840:

The island differs in many respects from the more northern, though the distance between them is only a few miles. The cultivation of the land is better and the crops almost suffice for its inhabitants, who, it is remarked, differ in dress and language from the others, are more active, industrious and consequently in better circumstances.

The islands, from their exposed and remote situation, have often been invaded by pirates and plundered of cattle, the natives usually contriving to save themselves among the high rocks. These robbers were not unfrequently French, English or Irish, a band of whom are said on one occasion to have been attacked and destroyed by the Suduroy natives.

The people of Faroe are still found to have retained the characteristics of their Scandinavian ancestors. The greatest difference is in the southern islands, whose natives have a rounder face, speak more rapidly and are more lively in their motions than those in the north.

It is here, on Suduroy, where Pal Joensen's story begins. An island of 'maybes' this is most certainly not.

**

Pal was ten when he first outlined his dream of becoming a swimming world champion. The Joensens were driving to their summer house and, sitting beside his father, Pal told his father, Kaj, that 'when I grow up I will be the champion in swimming'.

Kaj – his name is pronounced 'Kye' – stopped the car. He turned to Pal and asked him if he really meant what he had just said. Pal nodded. Since that day, as any father might, he has believed that Pal can be the best. 'I can't swim but I can help you as long as it takes. But I can't be in the pool,' he told his son.

It was the look in his eyes that had first given Kaj the belief in his son. 'Pal doesn't remember that episode, but I can recall it ir if it were yesterday. Since that day, he has totally meant to be a big swimmer.'

Pal was a quiet boy. He had friends, but was by no means a wild child. He was an easy son to deal with, according to his mother. He tried to play football and other sports, but didn't take to it. One day, when Pal was aged six, his parents told him to partake in another sport to keep himself occupied. He took to swimming on his first day in the pool.

The Joensens live in a traditionally modern Faroese house, nestled on the hills 200 metres above Vagur, one of the two largest towns in Suduroy, with bright windows and views of the fjord – but with no grass-turfed roof. It was a happy childhood for Pal. Meals were simple, mainly fish and boiled potatoes, peeled at the table. 'Not that much stands out,' he says.

Pal's parents had grown up on Suduroy. His father had been a seaman for twenty-five years and is now a marine engineer. He is the founder of a small firm, spending six years working hard on the project at home. Kaj was a chief engineer building a ship and couldn't find a proper solution to dealing with oily contaminated bilge water. Working long, arduous hours, he soon left to figure out this conundrum. With no income coming in, he developed a system which would pre-clean the contaminated water before ships put it overboard.

He calls himself 'a bit crazy', but the Edinburgh publisher's 1840 travel account of Suduroy is correct in its description of the Suduroy outlook: Kaj is more industrious than crazy.

Pal, meanwhile, was beginning to swim more and more on a regular basis. His local swimming club, based at a 12.5m pool in Vagur, had recently started up again. They had teamed up with a neighbouring club after a few barren years with no activity. But the situation was hardly ideal: twenty swimmers sharing a 12.5m pool which was only five metres wide.

Several older swimmers in Vagur had begun to take the sport more seriously. However, in that first year, some didn't find the sport as arresting as Pal, who kept turning up for sessions, kept turning in the small pool: 'I'm pretty happy that I held my own back then.'

Pal first started competing aged nine, three years after he first started to swim. The competitions started increasing as he got older, but the Vagur club didn't win many events when they travelled from Suduroy to the main islands. They just didn't have the experience of racing and winning meets. The training sessions at Vags Svimjifelag still lacked a serious edge, while coaches came and departed.

Swimming was interspersed with playing outdoors with friends. One day, he and two others went out in a motor dinghy, which one of his friends had recently procured.

The sea was choppy and the dinghy flipped. It was cold, the sea doesn't get warmer than around six degrees Celsius, but they managed to cling on to the boat for twenty minutes before, luckily, a passing car spotted the trio and help soon arrived.

It was a scary moment, but Pal remains nonplussed by the episode. He took diving lessons after getting an offer to do it for free. He didn't like the sea before and he hasn't swum in the sea since; it's just too damn cold: 'When you're swimming out there, there is the thought of what is down below or the stormy weather. When I was a kid, I didn't want to travel. It was always by a small, horrible boat and everyone got seasick the whole time and you were probably in bed the next day recovering.'

In the cosier environs of the indoor pool, Danja Martin Hofgaard, a childhood friend, stuck through the regime changes at the club. But, nearly two years older than Pal, Danja soon left swimming when he was fifteen. In 2015, Pal's friend – they both hail from the same small street of

Skalabeiti in Vagur – went on to become a world champion in another indoor discipline when he won the CRASH-B Sprint World Indoor Rowing Championships in Boston, USA.

A corner was eventually turned when Pal was fourteen. A new coach, Johan Martin Thorseinsson, who had worked as a carpenter, came to Vagur. For Pal, it was time to shape up, not least when Vagur became one of only three places in the whole of the Faroes to have a 25m, four-lane pool.

'I liked competing,' Pal recalls. 'The first time I think was in breaststroke at a 12.5m short course pool in the east of the island. I had a lot of friends who also swam in the team but they began to do other stuff. It was just for fun, hardly competitive, but as the swimmers got older, the coaches got a bit better. Johan gave new input to the team and he was the first full-time coach we had. He got my friend who quit to return to swimming and that year was one of the most fun times I could have had.

'For us, we felt as if we were getting more professional. Perhaps Jon [Bjarnason, his future coach] would say differently before he moved there, but in Faroese standards we had moved a lot. Until that point, other teams were kicking our asses. But now, we started to believe in ourselves and we began to win medals at the Faroese Championships.'

It was at the pool, when the two local clubs merged in Vagur, that Pal first met his childhood sweetheart and future wife, Malan. She was also a swimmer and they started training together around 2006, having not really spoken to each other prior to then.

That same year, Thorseinsson moved on after breathing life back into Suduroy's swim team through his volunteering. He wasn't an educated coach, but enthusiasm had been ingrained into his charges, who had now been engaged into their sport. He had built up a small team with some decent swimmers. There was now a foundation and parents were thankful.

In his place came a former Faroese swimmer, Jon Bjarnason, who had left the islands for Denmark. In an eight-year spell he had gained a graduate degree in coaching and coached in three different swimming clubs.

'When I was swimming we didn't even have a coach,' Bjarnason says. 'Actually my best times were done when I quit swimming, when I started teaching and realised how horrible my technique was. I improved a lot on my times and experimented with new techniques.'

Bjarnason first came across Pal when he was fifteen, five years after telling his father that he wanted to become world champion.

If Pal was going to realise his world title ambitions, he would have to overcome the inadequate facilities at Vagur: swimming and turning in a confined space, usually with younger locals splashing around in the next-door lanes.

The Faroes had just picked its squad for the Island Games, a biannual multi-sports event for member islands held in such diverse places as Rhodes, Isle of Wight, Bermuda and Jersey – and Pal had not been selected. 'He was useless and nobody saw any value in him,' admitted Bjarnason, when I first met him in May 2013.

I had travelled to Suduroy by boat, leaving port in Torshavn, with a sweeping panoramic of the capital. The maroon-coloured parliament building on the jagged rocks was the focal point. Grass-turfed houses were located behind, reminding me of Bill Clinton's remark when he had sent the Faroes into lockdown during a one-day visit to speak to local business leaders in 2007. The former US president claimed that if every building had greenery on its roof – it wasn't uncommon to see locals getting on top of theirs to mow or to see sheep grazing – then global warming would be greatly reduced.

Canada's biggest daily, the *Toronto Star*, had written at the time that Clinton's visit was 'the biggest news to hit the Faroe Islands since Christianity arrived about a thousand years ago'. Up on deck and leaving the capital behind, I wondered whether Pal's achievements, first garnered less than a year later, had achieved equal billing.

Thankfully, the government had purchased a second-hand naval boat which cut smoothly through the waters to Suduroy on a relatively calm day, as opposed to the previous old vessel where it was not uncommon for locals to be seasick.

I reached Vagur, passing little traffic, as the weather began to take a turn. Inside the pool, however, was a different matter. It was a hive of activity in the cramped and stiflingly hot four-lane pool. It was the first of two sessions, with junior swimmers putting in the hard graft ahead of the Faroese National Championships, a boat ride away back in Torshavn.

That evening, Jon, athletic and bald and with a determined face on pool deck, had invited me to his house a few minutes' walk from the pool. His parents had originally built the dwelling and had moved into the upstairs apartment while Jon's family had bought the ground floor. Over a veritable feast of meatballs, dips, sandwiches and copious amounts of tea, Jon laid bare those early days working with Pal.

They had first started talking about a seasoned plan in 2006. Prior to that, nobody had ever asked him about 'looking ahead' before. He was curious to know what the possibilities were.

But Suduroy needed a distance pool – Pal was swimming the longer events by now – and the strength training to go with it. What the pair really needed was dry land training space, but there simply wasn't the area for it at the club.

Only two swimmers could work out in a cramped area below the pool surrounded by piping, heating tanks and dripping roofs when it rained. It is a hot room, as you'd expect, but Pal did his best to work out here with body weights, push ups and chin ups.

'You have to believe or it's pointless working,' Jon told me. 'Everything starts with a dream and Pal wasn't afraid to think big. He knew that with these big dreams you had to work for it. It takes a special person to do what Pal does. Of course, there are now lots of kids who want to follow in his footsteps now.'

So is this ethos, the determination to succeed, consigned to the Suduroy people in the first instance?

'I find the people here to be much more different. They are more loud and open and the tempo is different. I'll say it is easier to find an athlete with the outgoing character of someone on this island. It is isolated and they are a different kind of breed.'

But Pal's character didn't fall into this category, at least at first.

From missing out on Island Games selection in 2005, Pal and Jon put in the hard yards. Pal started swimming close to 100 kilometres per week. Later, he was to manage over 120 kilometres per week, in 2010, but that was only because of a poor season the year before.

Pal would usually hit twelve kilometres every session. Jon then analysed his swimming, found his weak spots and worked him to the ground. The aim was to adjust his style and make him stronger.

'He was weak when he first started out. The girls on my team were stronger than him in strength training, which was obviously tough on him. Most guys wouldn't have been able to accept that. But he fought his way through it and took it as a challenge. That pretty much sums it up. I gave him a goal and he worked to succeed on in it.'

A few critics thought the pair's next plan – to travel to Melbourne to take in and experience life at the 2007 World Championships – was madness. 'Money up the wall at the bottom of the world' is how Jon describes the reaction to the idea.

But it was on this trip that Pal was catapulted to the elite junior stage.

One of the Faroes' many jaw-dropping landscapes

2

GLORIOUS DEFEATS

It is a near perfect spring Sunday evening in Torshavn. The harbour is calm and quiet, with the only sound being the gentle rattle of masts and a brilliant light coming off the sea.

In a nearby bar I am learning the history of Faroese swimming in finite detail, the country's previous sporting escapades and, of course, Pal's history and the admiration for the nation's undisputed number 1 sportsman.

I am with Rokur, a former swim coach turned IT professional, and his equally enthusiastic brother Bartal, a geologist. Rokur has travelled to swimming championships on holiday time away from his family, charted Pal's every move in the pool with thousands of images, and tried to get the Faroese media to show more interest in their star of the pool.

His love for the sport took him to working for the Faroese Swimming Federation, where he took over as president in 2014. Meanwhile, Bartal stayed at home and catalogued all of Pal's results, splits, times and medals. In all, it's a remarkable brotherly dedication towards one Faroese, who, one day, may or may not bring about a world title for this tiny population in the windswept North Atlantic.

At one point, Rokur tells me, 'Our heroism is really about the glorious defeats.'

For generations, children growing in the Faroes have been told old Norse stories of bold compatriots, but all ultimately ending with defeat. No tales of triumph here for children who have listened intently, a flicker of hope emerging, until the ending is revealed. Meanwhile, in sport, they've had to grow up with the efforts of the Faroese football team.

Undertaking extreme activities – rowing or swimming – is instilled into local folklore in these parts. In the 1900s there were stories of Faroese, especially women, doing marathon swims from island to island, which harks back to one legendary story told to every young Faroese by their parents.

It centres on Sigmundur Brestisson from the *Faereyinga Saga*, the only account about the history of the Faroes in the Viking era and early Middle Ages, which was written a couple of hundred years after the events took place.

According to the saga, the havoc created by Harald I of Norway had forced many to flee the country and settle in the Faroes around the beginning of the ninth century.

Some two hundred years later, Sigmundur was seen as the first Faroese to convert to the Christian faith and is thought to have created the first church on the islands in around AD 1000 at the behest of Olaf Tryggvason, the King of Norway, who was to become the Faroes' patron saint.

His family's stock had risen in the south, but pillagers from the north had nearly seen his farm and family wiped out. Sigmundur escaped, but was sent back to the Faroes to take possession of the islands for Tryggvason.

Undeterred, Sigmundur attempted to convert the islanders to Christianity but an unruly mob nearly saw him to his death. Together with a battle-hardened band of men, Sigmundur went one step farther. He travelled to the chieftain Trondur i Gotu's dwelling and in a night raid offered him a choice: either accept Christianity or face a beheading.

Having initially taken the former option, Trondur – who had 'a shock head of red hair … freckled of face and right grim of look' – then struck back a few years later with another night attack in Skuvoy.

Sigmundur and three others ran round the island, took a sixty-metre dive (I'd heard a few different accounts of this part, such is bedtime story-telling) over the cliffs and started swimming.

The Sandoy mountains were in sight for Sigmundur, but the tide began to take the trio towards Sandvik in northern Suduroy.

By this stage, his two increasingly wary companions could barely swim another stroke. The saga goes that Sigmundur swam on, though different tales suggest that he did so with one other, possibly his cousin, on his shoulders.

Exhausted and suffering from hypothermia after a long and cold swim, Sigmundur reached the beach and could barely move another muscle. A little while later, a local farmer, Torgrimur Illi (Torgrim the Mean), found the hulking figure on the beach. Torgrim lived up to his name when he saw a golden arm ring and killed the fatigued Sigmundur.

'It's a story of escape,' says Rokur. 'Every young child knows the story as it is the only written piece on Faroese history from settlement until the 1400s. He tried to save his friends but died from the physical challenge. That is a hero in Faroese culture and comes from one of the famous Viking tails. Apart from religion, there is nothing else that binds every Faroese household together.'

Even the British Armed Forces got in on the act with Faroese folk tales. With the German invasion of Denmark and Norway, Armed Forces were stationed on the Faroes throughout the Second World War in a friendly occupation known as Operation Valentine.

A publication was soon started up by the British, entitled *Fanfaroe*. In one edition I came across, the author, SK James, had written a tale called 'A Faroe folk legend'.

In the year AD 2543, a Faroe schoolmaster was telling a story at the annual Yol Fest (Christmas Tree). This was his tale.

Several hundred years ago, when the people of the world were less civilised than they are now, a war broke out between the nations of Europe. Soon most of the countries in the world were fighting. Although the Faroe folk were not at war, the people of England sent troops to the Faroes to prevent their enemies taking the islands and becoming a danger to Great Britain. Among the various types of troops sent up was what was then known as a battery.

This battery was stationed in a lonely fjord and for a long while guarded the entrance and watched for the enemy. But the enemy never came. Winds blew, storms rose, the waves clashed against the rocks and covered the watching soldiers with spray. But the enemy did not come.

Snow fell and ice formed. The watching soldiers were numbed with cold and their comforts ran short, but no enemy was seen.

For a long time, this battery kept its unceasing watch. The waters of the fjord were kept under constant observation and the skies were scanned diligently. Daily the men practised loading, aiming and firing their weapons, in pretence only, for they wished to conserve their ammunition against the time when the enemy should appear. But they did not come.

In this manner, the years slipped by and the battery maintained its continual watch. Although the war had been over and the fighting had ceased a long time previously, owing to a mistake this battery had been overlooked and had not been recalled. But they, unwitting of this change, still kept vigil.

As the years passed the men grew older. Their faces became wrinkled, their backs bent with age and their limbs stiff and feeble. Some lost the hair of their heads and became bald, while others ceased shaving and possessed beards that changed from grey to white as time went on.

They forgot why they were there and for what they kept watch, but still they mounted their guards and ever gazed seaward and skyward.

Some died and were buried by the guns they had tended. The remainder, old, grey and bent, went about their daily tasks as they had been accustomed. Fewer and fewer in number they became, older and more decrepit in appearance, and the people of the islands would come to the edge of the wire that surrounded their camp and gaze with wonder at these steadfast old men.

At length there came a time when there was but one left. He summoned himself to parades, checked himself as being present, detailed himself as lookout, ordered himself to perform the last rites known as the fatigues, mounted guard on the gate, and performed all the duties that had to be done. For he was a soldier and it did not enter his mind to vary the regular routine by one hair's breadth.

One day the people of the village noticed that the aged man was no longer to be seen crawling slowly from gate to guns, and from hut to the top of the lofty tower. They entered the camp and in a corner of the tall tower they found the stiff body of the last look-out, with antique binoculars clenched in his gnarled hands, gazing with sightless eyes for the enemy that had never come.

The good people of the village carried him tenderly from his post and with all the honour and reverence buried him with his companions beside the crumbling, rusting ruins of the antique weapons he had guarded.

And to this day the Faroe folk will tell you that on certain nights of the year at this place can be heard shrill noises, first three, then one, then shouting.

And there are those who say they have heard words and phrases like 'manning parade', 'markers', 'tell off', and other outlandish sayings.

People also say that they have seen ghostly figures running about and that fisher-folk at sea have seen spectral beams sweeping the surface of the fjord, and shadowy guns swinging slowly to and fro as the battery still watches for the enemy that will never come.

Some 100 years before Operation Valentine, households were few and far between. Until the 1830s there was only one store on the islands, in the capital Torshavn.

If you lived on the islands in the south, a once or twice yearly row was needed to stock up on supplies for the long months ahead. Failure to do so meant chancing your arm on merchants sneaking round the islands with untaxed goods. If you were caught, there were hefty fines to be paid.

Bedtime stories will have it that if one village boat saw another on one of these trips to the capital, they would seize the day and attempt to catch them. The craze caught on and soon villages were racing each other to see who could be the fastest and who was the strongest.

These rowing yarns are entwined with a real-life heroic adventure on the island, which, unsurprisingly, ends up as a heroic failure of sorts.

In the early 1980s, Ove Joensen, from the island of Nolsoy, a fjord's swim away from Torshavn, was earning his crust on a Danish training ship.

He climbed around on the frigate's rigs with apparent ease. Not a tall man, he was still as strong as an ox. But he soon returned to the Faroes to become a fisherman. He was the typical man at sea, too. When he went for a drink, he took out his roll of money, having earned his wage from weeks on the vessels, and would slowly dig into his savings.

However, Joensen had another agenda that he was plotting. In 1983, he announced to the editor of the local newspaper that he wanted to row the 900 nautical miles (1,700 kilometres) via the Shetlands Islands to Denmark.

His end goal was to row for a month and kiss the Little Mermaid in Copenhagen, but at the heart of the matter was raising funds so that Nolsoy could afford to build a new swimming pool.

He got his cousin to build a traditional Faroese boat, where he could sit in the middle and where it was covered at both ends. Painted across the stern was the boat's name, *Diana Victoria*, while there was a moderate mast stacked with running lights.

But for all his previous adventures on the high seas, remarkably, Joensen couldn't actually swim.

Not that it deterred him. He ended up attempting to row to Denmark twice – somewhere along the line he took his cat with him, but it fell over board and drowned – but being stranded in the Shetlands both times, where he allegedly got drunk and was sent home in disgrace.

A third time, in 1986, two years before the first Atlantic Airways flight from the Faroe Islands was scheduled to Copenhagen, he kept on rowing. Not that anyone would have turned up given his two previous attempts, but Joensen left the harbour without saying goodbye and started his quest.

He ended up in the centre of Copenhagen after forty-one days at sea and duly kissed the Little Mermaid. He became an instant hero, the Danish press hailing him 'Row Ove', as in 'row over'. Hundreds of ex-pats living in the Danish capital came out to welcome him home, while live TV pictures were beamed back to the Faroes.

Later, back in the Faroes, the 39-year-old was visiting his girlfriend on a neighbouring island, which naturally consisted of a small row across the fjord.

At the end of the day, no doubt well-fuelled with alcohol, he rowed back and, so the story goes, stood up to relieve himself at some juncture. He fell overboard and drowned. It was a barely believable end to his life considering he could stand on one leg at the top of masts, such was his balance on the high seas.

It was a sad, heroic end for a man who was well-loved. And who still is today, with fierce pride. In 2007, a *New York Times* journalist, Stephen Metcalf, ventured to Nolsoy, where he came across the *Diana Victoria*, still in fine condition.

Several locals from a nearby bar he had been drinking in followed the American hack outside, insisting on showing him Joensen's boat.

'The men around the *Diana Victoria* relay the story carefully, piece by piece, each detail of Ove Joensen's life laid out delicately, like a tiny wreath,' Metcalf wrote. 'They conclude by telling me, mostly in gestures, that after the journey, Joensen's hands never fully unfurled … In the interior gloom, the men's eyes glint with pride as their hands stroke the flanks of the rowboat. When I note how unusually small the blades of Joensen's oars are, one of the men snorts and says, "That's your problem. Why are your oars so big?"'

Joensen's grave at the village church has the inscription 'the fjord is rowed', while his headstone shows a black and white photograph of Joensen and the *Diana Victoria*. In honour of Joensen, the Faroes started an annual race, a four-kilometre swim across the fjord from Torshavn to Nolsoy.

If rowing wasn't the Faroes' most popular sport then, it certainly was now. It remained that way for another four years, until the Faroe Islands became a member nation of UEFA and competed in their first ever international football match on 12 September 1990, a qualifier for the 1992 European Championships.

Unfancied Faroes were pitted against Austria, fresh from their exertions at that summer's Italia 90 World Cup. Both sides had to travel for the game; the Faroes, the hosts of their first match, had no football pitch of note at the time.

Their surfaces were too rocky and hard and so the match was played in Landskrona, Sweden, with a small hardy band of Faroese support travelling over to take in a slice of history and, no doubt, a considerable thumping.

'Eighty per cent of the people at home told us that we were crazy to do this,' Faroes goalkeeper Jens Martin Knudsen, then a forklift truck driver in a fish factory, recalled two years' ago. 'We divided the match into five-minute intervals to help us overcome the competition. We considered it a huge success if we were able to restrain the Austrian team to only score five goals against us, we expected a 10-0 loss unless we broke the match into these smaller intervals. But before we know it, we are ahead in the game.'

Arni Gregersen, a TV journalist for Faroese broadcaster Sjonvarp Foroya, was commentating on the match and his live description (translated by a YouTube user) of the goal is majestic:

Ha ha, there is a panic among the Austrians... Here comes a long ball out on the wing... He can nearly reach it.

A cross, Jens Martin is up, here comes a shot again – and it's just off target. The biggest chance so far, yes. Kurt Russ, is regretting that, and he has every reasons for that.

And now it's Torkil... [some phrases here are difficult understand at this point because of the commentator's emotion]. AND SCORES! TORKIL NIELSEN SCORES! 1-0 TO THE FAROES! 1-0 TO THE FAROES! TORKIL NIELSEN FROM SANDAVAGUR! AIJAJAJAJAI! THE FAROES HAVE SCORED! TORKIL NIELSEN 1-0!

Oh, what wild jubilation here! Completely, completely, completely unbelievable how he managed to pass through all these men here. Helpless, they tried to drag his feet from under him. TORKIL SCORES! 1-0 to the Faroes. 1-0 to the Faroes. This goes against all expectations. Far, far, far, far from it.

So, the Austrians are in panic and are going to make substitutions. It is boiling here in Landskrona! Yes, if there hasn't been a panic among the Austrians before, there is now. Yes, what can you say after such a goal?

They returned to Torshavn as heroes after holding on for a hugely gallant 1-0 win; Nielsen showing that he was a two-pronged sportsman on the international scene after winning the Faroese National Chess Championships three times in the 1980s. Further, he returned to his girlfriend who had given birth to their first son just days prior to the Austria game.

And for Austria? As fanzine *When Saturday Comes* wrote in 2008, 'the impact of the match on the two countries could not have been more different. "The defeat put Austrian football back three years," midfielder Andreas Herzog has said. Josef Hickersberger, renamed "Faroer-Pepi" by the media, had to resign as coach the next day. Having been reappointed in 2005, one of his reasons for quitting again after Euro 2008 was that Austria had to travel to the Faroes in October for a 2010 World Cup qualifier. "I would have been shaking for a whole month ahead of the game," Hickersberger stated. "It was a personal tragedy for me, the bitterest moment of my career."'

So, how on earth had the Faroes' prevailed?

'I can, for instance, mention when I once trained with Arsenal for a week just before Christmas. There was a light breeze and perhaps some bits of snow and they had to cancel,' recalled Knudsen, famed for wearing a white skin-tight bobble hat during the win. 'This is considered good weather at home, and we would probably wear shorts for training. You can see it the way we play. We play hard, are strong and enduring. This is the reason we have been doing so well, despite being so small.'

By 'well', Knudsen meant competing against nations who had a far richer footballing pedigree – and with more players, too.

'It is the nature that shapes us and has given us the stubbornness that keeps us going. How can we otherwise challenge nations with two million players and we have only 1,500 footballers? It is because we believe in our own power, which is how we have survived the rough nature for centuries.'

Reading between the lines, the Faroes have quite clearly faced adversity with every international friendly and quali-fier they have played since 1990. Success has largely been absent, although there have been wins over the likes of Malta, San Marino, Estonia and Luxembourg.

Their finest win actually came in November 2014 when the number 187-ranked side in international football trav-elled to Piraeus and beat the might of Greece 1-0 in a Euro 2016 qualifier. Only their twentieth win ever, it forced an-other resignation for the losers. Defeat to the Faroes was seemingly intolerable. This time, Claudio Ranieri, the former Chelsea manager, took the bullet.

But what is the mood of the nation like when you are not a winning team? It was a question answered by the Faroes' Prime Minister, Kaj Leo Johannesen, whose Union Party took power after a swing to the right in 2011, when I met him at Logting. Translated as 'Law Thing', the Parliament house looks a traditional wood building structure from the outside, but has a thoroughly modern interior. There are glass tables, it's airy, bright and Scandinavian looking, with some officials working while standing up on Apple Macs.

'How do you make a nation proud when you have no chance of winning? It is easy to support them when it was good like in 1990,' says Johannesen, referring to efforts imparted by the Faroes' football outfit.

Johannesen made 300 appearances for local side Havnar Boltfelag as goalkeeper. He was part of the international side for six years and made eight appearances for the Faroes, including being on the bench for that fabled Austria game.

'I began to play football aged six. I had the privilege to play for my country. I was also part of the good games – in the days against Austria. 1990 was one of the biggest successes in soccer history. We didn't have any grass pitches back then and had to train on hard rock grounds before that. For the Faroes it was crucial as since then we have had a much more serious attitude towards football and sport. But now we come to the real hero and that's Pal.'

A character who could unite the people and youth of the island.

Pal celebrates gold at the 2008 European Junior
Championship, his first success

3

SEEDS OF SUCCESS

In the summer of 2006, Jon Bjarnason handed out a dose of reality to his elite junior swimmers at the club in Vagur, with some frank words.

'We were too weak and skinny and Jon told us so,' recalls Pal. 'Our balance was off and we had to start from scratch.'

At the following year's Nordic Junior Short Course Championships, held in the Faroes for the first time in several years, Pal came to the fore. Together with compatriot Kari Hovdanum, the pair recorded six national records, Pal setting a range of freestyle marks in the 200 metres, 400 metres and 1500 metres.

It was the first time that the Faroes had won even a single medal at the championships after previous domination from superior swimming nations, Sweden and Denmark.

'I knew that the next year was the 2008 European Junior Championships and I said I wanted to get medals. We looked at results from every other swimmer in Europe, comparing myself to others and their times and trying to get better than them.'

After Jon's 'weak and skinny' remarks, Pal then laid it out to his coach: just tell me what I have to do to get on the podium. 'I was sure that if I did it, I would improve and it would go a long way to making me a world champion.'

Soon, Pal and Jon worked for Pal to become the best distance swimmer in his age group. There wasn't anything new added to Pal's training, but the most striking addition came in the form of an oxygen tent, thanks to some sponsorship money trickling in.

Pal was effectively sleeping at altitude in his bedroom. 'I just got a lot of support, having become the first Faroese to win a medal at the Nordic Juniors. My girlfriend, Malan, gave me a lot of support and understood I had to sleep in a tent every night!'

After the championships, Pal also started rowing in six-man traditional Faroese boats. He was beginning to enjoy the social side of life on Suduroy as his confidence grew in the pool, and he was gaining muscle with each passing month. Not only that, he also improved his times by about twenty seconds in the distance events throughout 2007.

Still, by the time of the 2008 European Juniors in Belgrade, no one was expecting anything from Pal.

Yet, he defied the odds, swimming brilliantly to take an opening 400m freestyle gold, touching 0.11 seconds ahead of an Italian, a nation he was to battle with in later years at senior level on the European circuit.

Pal then doubled up his golden tally with a stunning 1500m freestyle swim, winning by over six seconds, meaning that the whole of the Faroe Islands was now on tenterhooks. They were expecting a third gold when the 800 metres was set to be raced on the final day of the championships.

Back on Suduroy, meanwhile, plans were put in place to set up a widescreen TV so that the village could all watch together. They soon had to resort to plan B when they couldn't find a feed from Serbian TV. Thus it was that a transistor radio with one speaker was placed in the middle of the village hall so that they could hear proceedings take place over 3,000 kilometres away.

While Pal swam the 800 metres, silence was ordered so they could trace the race, but the Suduroy people are an emotional bunch. It was going to be a hard task keeping them in check. It must have been some sight.

Initially, Faroese radio had decided not to broadcast the European Juniors, coming to the editorial decision that Pal was a long shot at best, coupled with the fact that the swimming federation was at odds with the national broadcaster at the time.

But thanks to a last-minute decision by a rival private broadcaster, Rokur travelled out, as part fan, part press attaché, part commentator: 'They just didn't believe it was possible [for Pal to win].'

With two golds banked already, a six-hour broadcast was made for Pal's final event – the Prime Minister was in the studio back in Torshavn – as he attempted to win a hat-trick of golds, an unprecedented moment for the Faroe Islands in the offing.

Rokur's brother, Bartal, remembers the moment when Pal 'hit the big time'. He could barely pull himself away from the TV but he had to go out shopping as Pal's race neared. When he reached the local mall, two boys were pumping the crackling radio feed out of the tannoy speakers at full volume, ironically some fifty metres away from the Faroes' national broadcasting HQ.

The final was at 5pm and the mall was now filled with people. The race was going well.

Faroes Commentator 1 (Jon Bryan Hvidtfeldt): Something has to go really, really, really wrong here for Pal.

Faroes Commentator 2 (Rokur): Nothing can go wrong, nothing can go wrong, it is not possible. Even if he swims easy he has won.

At the end of a deathly quiet eight minutes, as Hvidtfeldt, the only journalist in Belgrade, described Pal to the wall for gold, grown men burst out crying on Suduroy. On touching, Pal turned, saw the scoreboard as well as his time and hit the water hard with his palm in celebration. 'When I had 500 metres to go, when I saw I was so far ahead, I began to sing the national anthem in my head,' Pal said.

The biggest moment yet in Faroese sporting history had arrived (perhaps barring the Faroes' win over Austria – no doubt a hot topic of debate in pubs across the archipelago). Finally, adults had a new bedtime story to tell their off-spring. Heroic failures? Pah!

'I reasoned, and publicly announced, that this would be a sure win, as he had already won the 400 and 1500 metres,' recalls Rokur. 'The private radio station went "all in", previewing and then broadcasting pretty much all day. We were live from Belgrade, thanks to a Nokia phone, from before the finals and until a couple of hours after.

'In the radio studio, congratulatory text messages were read out and there were people including the Prime Minister there too. We had a long talk with coaches Jon Bjarnason and Petur Heoin a Flotti at the pool, after the final session. And we talked with people live during the final session. Pal's parents, his brother, anyone we could find. It was a great day.'

With all this hoopla, Faroese heroism of sorts had already made its mark after Pal's opening gold in the 400 metres: the organisers couldn't find a Faroe Islands flag to hoist in between the Italian and Great Britain colours.

'This chance, that a small country would win gold was clearly beyond the Serbian organisers,' laughs Jon Hestoy, the former Faroese Swimming Federation president. 'Someone ran up to the stands to ask Pal's parents if they could borrow their flag.'

One by one, the flags were hoisted up. The Union Jack for bronze, Italian for silver and then, what looked like the size of a table napkin in comparison, the Faroese flag, hanging joyfully in the middle.

The following day, the organisers got their thinking caps on and had one at the ready for Pal's second medal. Hestoy doesn't know to this day how they managed to obtain this small island's flag. 'Perhaps from an embassy,' he says. 'When you come to a major championships, you have to sign that this is your anthem and your flag. But this picture, you wouldn't believe it. If nobody had a flag on the stands, of course there wouldn't have been one in the middle.'

Rumours began to emanate from Suduroy that a welcome reception was going to take place for Pal's heroic return. On the flight back to Torshavn, it was announced that Pal was on board. He was invited to sit in the cockpit and generally lavished with praise as the sweeping mountains came into view.

As the plane touched down, the water cannons burst into life, creating an aquatic arch for the returning champion. Pal stepped out onto Faroese soil, complete with the red carpet treatment. He was overcome with emotion.

After a reception in the capital, there were further jovialities on the boat to Suduroy. At this point, success felt normal to Jon and Pal as they had experienced the winning feeling at Nordic Junior Championships.

'But this was much bigger and we didn't really think about it,' says coach Bjarnason. 'We were laughing and talking on the ferry before fellow passengers said we had to go out on deck and see the waiting party in port.'

As news had filtered through of Pal's docking time, so the harbour was soon filled with islanders and cars. As the boat rolled into port, the sense of achievement hit home again for Pal and Jon.

'It came to us really hard. I remember looking over at Pal, who had this empty expression on his face. Tears were streaming down his cheeks.'

Every single motorbike on the island seemed to be in attendance while cars were spread all over the port terminal. There were fireworks too, and it took some time just to move on and continue onwards to Vagur. A few miles out, they transferred from cars on to the back of an open truck. A convoy of motorbikes rode in front and behind with Faroese flags.

It's at this point, with Bjarnason reminiscing over what the pair talked about on the back of the truck, that he harks back to Pal's schooldays.

He remembers speaking to some of his teachers, asking them what kind of pupil Pal was. He wanted to know how he was progressing in school, before he looked to take on Pal for twelve sessions per week in the pool. Did he have any problems? Was he a listener? 'Oh, just go ahead,' the teachers told the coach. 'He will never be anything really. He will go out to sea like his father. He's not a book person.'

'I remember telling this to Pal before he wanted to become European junior champion.' Bjarnason recalls. 'His work ethics were amazing. He went from being a low-achiever to the best in his class and moving on to high school and being the best there. So, thank you teachers!

'He's not very outspoken and he always came across as a shy person when I first met him. So he found it difficult to react on the back of that truck. He wasn't used to receiving that much adulation. I told Pal on the docks when we returned to suck up the moment and don't be afraid to show emotions. It's okay to do this.'

Dressed in his blue Faroese swim team outfit alongside his coach, the pair were holding on to the sides of the trailer, with the Suduroy wind in their faces. It was an immensely good feeling and, again, it proved too much for Pal as the convoy drove past a fish factory in his village. All the workers, complete in their white outfits, had come out to wave and congratulate Pal.

Eventually, they ended up at the local football club, with more cake, more speeches. 'And then came the evening,' says Rokur of a party which lasted long into the night, one involving traditional songs, three especially written for the seventeen-year-old champion.

'When it was all over in Belgrade, I was overjoyed but didn't think too much about it,' says Pal. 'It's when I got home that it really hit me. How much support and how glad and happy people were for me. The coverage of the event was really good and everybody came out to see me. When we came back, they said we weren't going in a car or a bus, you are going on this thing here. Everybody was out waving, the fish factory closed for half an hour and they came out on to the road.

'The feeling was so special. You don't think of how big it is when you are away, but we had it when we beat Austria.

The whole islands were out to greet us when we came back. Then you realise, oh my god, that it's much bigger than I thought, one minute after finishing my swim. It is a whole country coming together, cheering you on to gold. That is one of the best pictures I can recall on the truck. It was pretty tough afterwards. I wanted to set new goals, but I felt like I couldn't live up to or impress people the same way. I didn't really feel the same urge to get people's acceptance as an athlete as I had already proved it to them.'

There would be more accolades to come, but Belgrade was the biggest as far as the Joensen family were concerned. It was first time that he had showed what he could do at international level. Excitement naturally grew within the Faroese swimming community.

It was a big change for Pal, but he got used to it. Slowly he started training again – and improving. To such a degree that by the time Christmas came about, he was a sure favourite to take the Faroese Sportsperson of the Year award.

No one had expected anyone to overshadow Katrin Olsen, the rower who was forced to switch nationalities to Denmark so that she could become the first Faroese to compete at the Olympics (she reached the semi-finals in the lightweight double scull in the Beijing Games).

She may have lost her Island Games status, but changing countries was the only option left to her thanks to the International Olympic Committee failing – and still failing – to recognise the Faroe Islands as a member country.

It was a scenario that was to befall upon Pal as he stepped up a gear to world-class level ahead of the London 2012 Games.

For now, Pal's bounty in Belgrade had lifted swimming to new heights. He lifted the New Year's Eve accolade for three years in a row until the broadcaster scrapped the annual award to save money. Comically, after a few years, they reintroduced the Footballer of the Year award instead.

But it goes without saying that Pal was now the biggest sportsman on the islands. It was even on tape, Rokur told me, where a Faroese footballer was asked whether a recent performance a few years ago was the best thing to happen on the island. 'No no, no,' he responded. 'There is Pal, and then there is us!'

Pal enjoyed a fruitful relationship with his coach,
Jon Bjarnason

4

ROAD TO LONDON

When Jon and Pal travelled to Melbourne for the Faroes' first taste of a World Championships this century, there were detractors who didn't think much of the idea.

But by entering into every single freestyle event, Pal was primarily there to gain experience. In a rare feat, the Faroese participated in a Michael Phelps-like five events, though stretched out over the full set of disciplines: 50m, 100m, 200m, 400m, 800m and 1500m freestyle events.

Pal failed to emerge through the heats of each of his races, but racing tough against the world elite had now been rubber-stamped in his swimming passport.

The following year, a few months after his heroics in Belgrade, Pal broke the fifteen-minute barrier over 1500 metres, with a time of 14:49.34 at the Danish Short Course Championships, winning by over twenty-seven seconds.

At the time, the Danish Swimming Association allowed the Faroese to set Danish records, perhaps figuring that their swimmers wouldn't be able to set any. Pal's time was duly recorded.

The following week, the Danes seemed to have a change of tack, noting that the Faroes now had such a strong swimmer. For, shortly afterwards, the ruling was overturned and the Danish junior record was reverted back to Mads Glaesners' time from 2006 (14:50.72), which still stands today.

I can't help but wonder whether Pal had been stymied so early in his career by the Law of Jante, or *jantelagen*, the concept taken from a book by Aksel Sandemose, the Danish-Norwegian author who died in 1965. I had heard the phrase used several times in reference to Pal's career in the Faroes, with the Jante Law discouraging Scandinavians from promoting their own achievements over others. Still prevalent in modern society, 'You are not to think you are anything special' is one of the ten commandments. Pal was, essentially, 'average man'.

Undeterred by this small setback, Pal had firmly stepped up from junior level and was now ready for Rome and his second major meet, the 2009 World Championships.

However, these championships were to go down into the record books for all the wrong reasons. They proved a seismic disaster for the integrity of the sport and left Mark Schubert, USA Swimming's national team director, to remark: 'This will be remembered as the plastic meet.'

Over the course of a toxic week in the pool at the Foro Italico, swimmers set forty-three world records in what was to prove the last major meet to use 'super suits'.

The Speedo LZR Racer swimsuit, made of fifty per cent polyurethane and designed alongside NASA scientists, had hit the market in February 2008 and was responsible for eighty-odd world records as the World Championships got under way a year later in Rome. At the Beijing Olympics, the LZR was behind a ninety-four per cent winning ratio of all races in the pool and eighty-nine per cent of all medals.

With no stitching down the side of the suit, it added a new dimension to streamlining. Then along came copycats such as the Adidas Hydrofoil and, from the Italian manufacturer, the Jaked suit, which was 100 per cent polyurethane. It was totally water repellent, no air could get out, meaning swimmers stayed buoyant and produced less drag.

As Louise Burke, an Australian sports scientist, remarked at a sports medicine meeting in San Francisco in 2012, 'The fast suits were kind of like the Spanx of swimming. They put everyone in to the right shape for swimming, and allowed for swimmers with different body types.'

Compressed suits such as these had downsides to the blistering times being set in the pool: they took about thirty minutes just to get into the thing. Changing rooms in 2009 must have been a comical sight, with fellow swimmers helping each other get into costumes.

The phrase 'technological doping' was soon being bandied around. After passing through a succession of fast suits, FINA, swimming's world governing body, soon saw the light and high-performance non-textile wear was banned the following year, though the records set in Rome would last a good deal longer (only two world records were set prior to the London 2012 Olympics).

Rebecca Adlington, double Olympic champion, had refused to wear the 'shiny suit' as *The Times* swimming correspondent Craig Lord dubbed it, despite her rivals, including compatriot and fellow freestyler Jo Jackson, doing so.

'I think it's a shame to be honest,' Adlington, then twenty, told BBC Sport in 2009. 'Swimming always used to be a level playing field.'

If Pal was hoping to make inroads in Rome, he was to be sorely disappointed. The disparity in the pool, in both times and performances from the haves and have-nots of the shiny suits, left the sport divided.

Pal had never felt comfortable in the fast suits. Whenever there was a new one on the market, swimmers flocked to keep up with the latest developments. 'It was a crazy, stupid time and best to be forgotten,' says Bjarnason, 'and I hope FINA never go down that road again.'

The fast suits had even filtered into competition swimming at the European Juniors the previous summer. In the 400 metres, Pal found himself swimming against rivals who had swimsuits on with the latest fancy names, though he had opted for a normal kneeskin suit.

Pal had already tried on the suits, but there was no doubt in his mind that he was going to win European Junior gold that day. He was to soon find out that the suits were best suited to those swimmers with a good kick, which Pal didn't have.

The Rome championships saw the Suduroy swimmer fail to make it past the heats of any of his events. He qualified seventeenth-fastest in the 1500 metres, with 15:21.37, some three seconds slower than his gold-medal swim as a junior in Belgrade.

He sat in the bus ferrying swimmers back to the team hotels and shook his head in disbelief at how swimmers could go so fast. He was shell-shocked, especially after he had won eight golds and six silvers at the Island Games (featuring few world-class athletes) earlier in the year.

Still, Pal's rise had seen him awarded a grant by the Faroes' powers-that-be. It was a new concept as far as Faroese sport was concerned, and, unsurprisingly, there were those who questioned it. Thus, it was important to deliver on the funding.

He cast aside his Rome disappointments with a successful season in the 25m short course pool. At the FINA World Cup series meetings in Moscow, Berlin and Stockholm, Pal won gold and two silvers over 1500 metres, setting new Nordic records in the process.

**

From a British point of view – well, for the meagre three British journalists who were there at any rate – the 2010 European Championships in Budapest were likely to yield few medals, given that the team went into the biannual event 'unrested'. The Commonwealth Games in Delhi were looming and times were likely to be erratic throughout the squad. However, judging by Hannah Miley's swim for Great Britain on the opening night, the championships would paint a different picture.

The venue, Margaret Island on the River Danube, had a capacity of around 5,000, and when a local Hungarian was in any race, there was quite a din. Not least with the sound of the vuvuzelas, which had now entered into the sporting psyche following the summer's football World Cup in South Africa.

The cacophony was silenced following a devastating burst of speed on the breaststroke leg – her third 100 metres – as Scotland's Miley, all 5 feet 4 inches of her, came from a body length down on local favourite Katinka Hosszu to open up a two second gap going into the final freestyle. She won in 4:33.09, a championship record, leaving Hungary's world champion over three seconds adrift.

With clear daylight between the pair, it was nearly five seconds before Miley took off her goggles and turned round to face the scoreboard, raising both arms aloft. It was a marvellous swim and left her dad and coach, Patrick, who was also a North Sea helicopter pilot, in tears behind the scenes.

His charge had never won a major title before (she finished fourth at the 2009 World Championships in Rome) and he admitted to not knowing the winner's protocol. 'She is an inspiration to me and I'm her coach,' he said.

By the time Sunday came along, some five days after Miley's opening gold, Britain was in the ascendancy and the image of the championships, from a British perspective, saw Fran Halsall, the bubbly Plato and Aristotleloving swimmer from Southport, drape the Union Jack behind her shoulders after Great Britain finished with a record eighteen medals overall.

Over the course of a week at a swimming meet, journalists get a real sense of the pressure some swimmers are under to perform, especially if they are competing in more than one discipline. This applied to Adlington, who was left in tears after finishing seventh in the 800 metres, but came back superbly to take 400m gold, her first major title since her Beijing brace.

Amidst all this came Pal. With no Brits on the 1500 metres final start list, I had come across the Faroe Islands entry as he surged into an early lead. Surely this was no Eric the Eel tale.

'I tell you, Belgrade was big, but Budapest was bigger in terms of making your mark and Pal doing it on the international stage at a senior meet,' Hestoy recalls three years later at a restaurant in Barcelona during the World Championships. 'His swim in Budapest was blistering. He charged from the off and he had half a pool length on the others.'

Pal, one of only two finalists who had never raced a major final before, did indeed go out at a decent pace. The Italian Samuel Pizzetti tried to go with him and, lurking in third, was Sebastien Rouault, of France.

While Pal was 'going like a machine', the wise Rouault was letting Pizzetti do all the work in front of him.

At 500 metres, Pal had a healthy lead. By the 1,000-metre turn, he held a two second lead. With 200 metres left, four lengths to go, the Frenchman attacked. And by the next turn he was tied with Pal.

'There was a kind of a rabbit and hare race going on,' Hestoy recalls. 'The Italian was the rabbit for the French guy. It was kind of team work. He was the smart guy. Pal was the crazy guy and Pizzetti was just ambitious. Pal was keeping the distance and the speed. It was unbelievable and everything was perfect. He couldn't have done it any other way but he just didn't have the sprinting power at the end.'

The Frenchman, who had nearly quit the sport in the aftermath of the 2009 fast suit controversy, pounded his legs down the finishing straight and took gold in the fastest time in the world so far that year, 14:55.17. Pal touched in 14:56.90, a new Nordic record.

'Joensen is not yet twenty. What he lacks in age, he more than makes up for in courage,' Craig Lord wrote at the time on *SwimNews*, which is now effectively *SwimVortex*. 'The young brave from the Faroes, coached by Jon Bjarnason, had lost gold but what a worthy silver medallist and a great hope for the future.'

And then came the killer line from Lord, one that was to spark a meeting of minds back on Suduroy, turning into reality some five years later. 'Faroe Islands: build that man a 50m pool and name it after him…'

The silver sparked another evening of celebration for the small Faroese contingent on Margaret Island.

'It was a fantastic evening nonetheless,' recalls Hestoy. 'When you go out at that speed, you are afraid he might break but he never did that. The way he swam it was so convincing, the stroke and everything. The French guy was swimming like crazy for the last 400 metres. At the end, we were drinking champagne and even the French joined in and gave a speech. In the evening, we went up to a hotel room and drank whisky with the French national coach. It was really fantastic.

'It wasn't an anti-climax because he created that competition all the way through. He just went out and left the field, controlling the race. After Budapest, I was sure that, money wise, our federation was saved thanks to his European medals. We really had had a hard time translating that success into sponsorship. You would think that anyone, any company would have wanted to use Pal's name as a byword for success.'

Pal's times and silver in Budapest left the Faroese in confident mood as the short course season loomed. But there was to be disappointment in Dubai at the 25m World Championships that December, a meet where he was hoping to become world champion.

By this time, the national television broadcaster had produced a documentary on Pal's career to date, with the programme stating that he was set to become the world's best.

He was focused, but by his own admission he was holed up in his hotel for too long before the meeting. Perhaps he was too relaxed, for he failed to reach the final and was some ten seconds off a top eight berth.

Two heats later, however, came a moment which emulated the feats of the Equatorial Guinean, Eric 'The Eel' Mousambani, at the 2000 Sydney Olympics.

Jackson Niyomugabo, a 22-year-old Rwandan swimmer and stalwart of the 2008 Beijing Olympics, took over twenty-three minutes to complete his race, some nine minutes off qualification. With swimmers ready for the next discipline, Niyomugabo was freestyling for nearly six minutes until he thought he had finished.

The pool judges told him that he still had a few more lengths to go, so he bravely plundered on until he touched the wall to enthusiastic applause from the locals. 'I will train hard to improve,' Niyomugabo, who learnt his art from a French book called *The Secrets of Swimming Development* despite not speaking the language, told reporters afterwards.

Pal's own development saw him arrange a training camp with the Icelandic swim team in Singapore as the long course World Championships loomed the following summer.

Pal's career had seen him travel to meets alone, or with his coach Jon, but as each season passed so he built up his network of friends. His closest on the circuit was Alexander Dale Oen, a likable and outgoing Norwegian, who had won breaststroke silver at the Beijing Olympics.

The two struck a chord as their careers blossomed, while Dale Oen, who was a few years older, was to enjoy a difficult but ultimately fruitful World Championships.

Pal and Dale Oen were staying at the same hotel in Shanghai when, on 22 July, Anders Behring Breivik killed 77 people and injured 242 more in gun and bomb attacks in Oslo and on the island of Utoeya, a spree regarded as the worst act of violence in Norway since the Second World War.

Pal remembers sharing breakfast with his Norwegian friend, who had obviously spent most of the night glued to the television to keep abreast of events. 'He was shocked but I could sense that he was still focused on what he was going to do in the pool.'

Three days after the massacre, Bergen-born Dale Oen won 100m breaststroke gold, dedicating the win to the victims and pointing to the Norwegian flag on his cap on taking the title.

However, a further tragedy was to strike the Norwegian swim team the following May.

Seen as one of the London Olympic's medal favourites following his gold in China, Dale Oen, still only twenty-six, died suddenly of a suspected cardiac arrest while attending a high-altitude training camp in the United States.

He was found collapsed in a shower after having earlier undergoing a light training session and a round of golf in Flagstaff, Arizona. He had been in good spirits. Having returned from injury, he was looking ahead to the Olympics and had been planning a hiking holiday in Scotland following London 2012.

For Pal and the swimming community, it was a total shock: 'A lot of people would say that they knew Alex pretty well. He always talked to a lot of people in the sport and the reason why I got to know him was when I first started to go on long course training in Iceland.'

Their friendship developed by virtue of the fact that their two countries were low scale when it came to swimming as a whole, given Norway's penchant for excelling in winter sports.

'He was pretty much a pioneer in Norwegian swimming really. He thought outside the box and that's how he saw himself. He had a lot of inspiration from Arctic explorers and he was interested in those aspects and how they survived.'

As Pal began to understand the swimming community, he slowly began to talk to other swimmers, not just relying on his small team of coach and sometimes mother, who acted as a physio. In Dale Oen, he found common ground.

'We had a bond. He used to travel alone to events as well and I was pretty much lost when it came to international meets in the early days. International swimming is just a big club of people and I have tried to have fun with it as each year has passed. Alex was open. He would sit with me at lunch and integrate me with other swimmers. I think it was because he saw me as someone who was also from a small country.

'I come to know now some of his strengths, especially since I have gone back to Bergen, Alex's birthplace. We had a lot of competitions together. He was a really sweet guy and had an excellent mind set for a swimmer. I started idolising him more for his personality and his love of the sport. For a breaststroker, you can hardly compare that to a long-distance swimmer, but he became a mentor by the way he handled things. He loved swimming more than anything and I think that's why he became interested in my career, coming from an even smaller country, with even fewer athletes.'

Pal recalls Dale Oen telling him a story he had once told a Norwegian journalist in an interview. How, the reporter said, was it possible that a guy from a small town in Norway had become one of the best swimmers in the world? Dale Oen recounted the Frog Story.

How there was once a bunch of small frogs, who had organised a running competition. The aim was to reach the top of a very high tower and, as word had spread, so a big crowd had gathered to see the race unfold.

No one in the crowd really believed that the tiny frogs would reach the top of the tower. They shouted 'way too difficult', 'the tower is too high'. The frogs began collapsing, one by one, except for those who were climbing higher and higher.

The crowd continued to shout that no one would make it. As more frogs got tired and gave up, one continued to go higher. He just wouldn't give up! And those at the top of the tower wanted to know how on earth this small frog has reached the top. The secret? He was deaf.

Not listening to the doom-mongers had been one of Pal's fortes, so he could relate to the tale and why Dale Oen had told him the episode with the journalist. He was proud of having someone to compare himself with in some way. He told Pal over lunches and evenings together about how he improved and gained experience, by training and communicating with other athletes.

'He was always happy and making people laugh. He talked to everybody and wasn't shy at all. He wanted to swim until he was an old man, he thought about nothing else. His death was such a sad story.'

Dale Oen's gold in Shanghai did, though, see Pal produce a phenomenal swim in his distance events. Having qualified second-fastest, he set a new Faroese and Nordic record in the 800m final in placing fifth.

Four days later he was back in another final, the 1500 metres, a race which saw Australian great Grant Hackett's ten-year world record – and the only one to survive the shiny suits fiasco – shattered by China's distance merchant Sun Yang in a time of 14:34.14.

Pal was right in the mix for medals as the race progressed before Sun raced away with gold. With 200 metres left, the Hungarian Gergo Kis caught Pal and the Faroese had to settle for fourth, less than a second behind. In a race like the 1500 metres, this must rank as one of the more dispiriting positions to finish in the sport.

However, there was salvation: he was some twenty-five seconds under the qualification time for London 2012. His swimming also proved a standout for European selectors ahead of Duel in the Pool, the Ryder Cup-style meet against the USA, with Pal being picked for the distance events.

Three years on from his Belgrade performances, Pal's tale was beginning to capture the imagination of the swimming community.

Following Pal's Duel in the Pool selection, Rokur wrote on his swimming blog: 'Baby steps, baby steps, but actually huge steps from the viewpoint of this baby. I did a calculation that showed that with our population of about 50,000 people, the odds are that there will be 12-13 years between each Faroese participant at the Olympic Games (in any sport), and 440-460 years between each Olympic gold medal. With Pal having a realistic chance of reaching the London 2012 final in the 1500m freestyle, you can imagine that this probability puts a bit of pressure of those of us in charge, that don't count on living for 500 years.'

Yet, for all his endeavours and hitting the Olympic mark, there were difficult choices to make if he was to realise his ambition of becoming only the second Faroese-born athlete to appear at the Games.

He would have to swim for a different country – and a non-Faroese flag on the side of his swim hat.

The outsider: Pal swimming for the Denmark team

5

THE HORRIBLE FLOP

Isolated from German-occupied Denmark in the Second World War, the British Armed Forces' occupation of the Faroe Islands meant that the small nation of eighteen islands was pretty much self-governed, barring military matters.

The Treaty of Kiel in 1814 had originally granted Denmark control over the Faroes, so when the war ended, the islands' political parties found themselves in a quandary as normality resumed.

The Faroese had been in favour of independence following a referendum in 1946, but the Danish government overturned the decision and the King dissolved parliament. Two years later a Home Rule Act was subsequently passed, which saw the islands become an autonomous, self-governing region of the Kingdom of Denmark.

As far as Faroese sport was concerned, letters and faxes began piling up some thirty years later. Firstly, the Faroese Confederation of Sports applied to FIFA, world soccer's governing body, and then UEFA, the European equivalent, to become a full member nation.

In 1984, the Faroes made contact with the International Olympic Committee to start the process of becoming an IOC member country. It was a slow procedure. Applications were sent, long waits for replies ensued. Responses came back seeking clarifications, then all communication died.

Some twenty years after first applying, the Faroese ministry sent another letter, this time with some strong backing. They had the support of the Danish Prime Minister and National Olympic Committee presidents from Norway, Iceland and Finland. It was a Nordic collective.

What rankled with the Faroese – they were already part of the Paralympic movement and could compete under the Faroese flag – was the way that their 1984 submission petered out, some two years before the IOC recognised National Olympic Committees being formed by Aruba, the Cook Islands and Guam.

'Not to put pressure on Pal, but it was one of the reasons why a success at London 2012 would have pressed the Faroese cause,' Hestoy says. 'The biggest problem for the IOC was that they didn't want to open the floodgate of countries pressing for IOC status.'

Since July 2007, an amendment in the Olympic Charter meant that non-independent countries could no longer become IOC members. Trying to hold even a meeting with IOC suits proved virtually impossible for the Faroes.

But Pal's rise in swimming had kick-started the Faroese Swimming Federation into life. FINA's previous rule meant that if you changed country there was a twelve-month exclusion from competing, meaning no Shanghai World Championships in 2011 and no London 2012 Olympics.

However, Pal's form on the world circuit started a process whereby FINA agreed that a swimmer could compete for his or her nation without being sanctioned with a one-year quarantine out of the pool. It was seen as a major breakthrough.

'It wasn't what we wanted as we weren't recognised as an IOC country,' Hestoy admits, 'but it was the best possible option. This meant that you could stay a Faroese swimmer – and it's better to be Danish for twelve days, than two years.'

So a passage had now been opened for Pal to compete at London 2012. But it was to be no simple one, at least in Pal's mindset. Fiercely patriotic to the Faroes, Pal had been adamant, a year out from the Olympics, that he would never change citizenship or swim for Denmark.

However, the Danish and Faroese federations acted as one. For the Faroese federation, the prospect of Pal ever swimming at the Olympics had looked but a distant dream, but suddenly a simple solution began to unravel.

For the IOC, it was never a problem, but FINA had to agree for Pal to be handed temporary citizenship for Denmark before competing as a Faroe Islander as soon as the

Olympics were over. In rare cases such as this, red tape usually takes on a life of its own, but the process turned out to be a relatively simple one. Pal was free to swim for Denmark.

Hestoy, with a grin emerging ever so slightly, says that Pal was now swimming for the 'Danish Kingdom'. 'It sweetened it just that little bit more, instead of Denmark! But, no, the Danes had been brilliant for Pal and did everything to make it possible. They have done so since 1984 when we first began our application to become a member of the IOC. Everything considered, it was a match made in heaven.'

**

Pal had a 'real nationalist feeling' when he was competing abroad with the Faroese flag emblazoned across his swim hat. He always talked about his island roots with other interested and like-minded swimmers and coaches.

Hailing from a small, traditional community, one not used to sports or Faroese breaking through onto the world stage for that matter, left a sense of pride within Pal: 'I still hold on to the island traditions and at the same time want to become a better sportsman. But if I was going to swim at the Olympics I had to swim for Denmark and switch nationality. I was told that the federations were talking. It was tough news to get as I was really optimistic about the Faroes getting IOC membership. But changing nationalities meant I got the best of both worlds. I got the funding and support of the people and then I can train in a long course pool with world champions and high-paid coaches. Every week there is a physio, massage and diet experts.

'At the same time, if I changed I would lose all that: my nationality drive and the push for the Faroes to advance in international swimming. I had proved that being an athlete from a small community, I couldn't impress people more. Of course, going to the Olympics as a Faroese would be the ultimate. But I concentrated on the positives of swimming for Denmark. The coaches, the setup, the results, meant I would learn a lot as most of them were much more experienced than me.'

Other athletes over the years had experienced far greater problems when it came to switching nationalities. In Britain, for example, Peter Nicol, the Scottish former world number 1 squash player, was pictured on the front page of *The Times* newspaper in 2001 when he opted to compete for England, a country with greater funding and training opportunities.

Swapping the Saltire for St George's cross had greatly affected Nicol when the decision was made, though he was to cast aside those early fears with Commonwealth Games gold in 2006.

Then came the 'Plastic Brits' controversy in the build-up to London 2012. A *Daily Telegraph* survey had revealed that eleven per cent of Team GB's 542-strong squad had been born abroad and as the *Daily Mail* newspaper went on the rampage, the fiasco forced the then-IOC president, Jacques Rogge, to seek clarity on this growing trend, but at the same time outlining his concerns.

'You have athletes who for absolutely legitimate reasons want to change nationality, because they get married, because they get a new job, because of studies,' said the Belgian in March 2012. 'You have a number of athletes who switch nationality mainly because there is absolutely no support or money available at the level of the sports ministries, there is no way they can get grants. These athletes want to change nationalities on the proposal of other countries. It is not what I love the most but I understand the needs of the athletes who want to develop their skills and who sometimes have family and professional and family responsibilities.

'Then you have those athletes where there is support for them but they go to another country because there is a bigger gain to be made. Legally we cannot stop this but it does not mean we love it. I have reservations in the cases of the athletes who obviously don't lack any support emanating from their sporting and government authorities and who still change nationality. We cannot oppose it because it is a matter of sovereignty but let me tell you frankly we do not love that.'

Pal, of course, was not opting to swim for Denmark for financial gain. He had reached a point of his career through sheer hard work. He had gone alone in a pursuit of not following the path of others. He had simply invested time and effort in something he was counting on that might benefit his future down the line.

He had started training with the Danes in 2012, but his build up to the Olympic dream really began back at the

2011 World Championships, where he had produced his best set of results and times in Shanghai.

His fourth place in the 1500 metres and fifth in the 800 metres were close to European records in both events. Expectations began to grow, though Pal hadn't been training that well due to a knee injury which was affecting his turns.

Attentions turned to the Olympics, as a swimmer, not as a Faroese athlete. He began to slowly learn from the Danish team, as a lot of them were 'big inspirations for me'.

There were training camps at high altitude in Canada and South Africa where Pal got to know the team and the coaches, while Jon was also coaching alongside. It felt less a Danish team, more an international one: the Tunisian swimmer Oussama Mellouli was there, while some of the coaches were Dutch.

The Danish squad had begun to use hypoxic tents to simulate high altitude and it was at one of these camps that a Danish physiologist recognised that Pal's key ingredient seemed to be his oxygen saturation, research revealing that Joensen had a higher oxygen count than anyone else.

Jon also recalls a moment in Sierra Nevada, Spain when the coaches all went out jogging. He couldn't understand why they were all gasping for air. 'And I was like "come on guys, what's up?" I believe that it must be something to do with our genetics.'

I'd heard many explanations as to why Pal excelled at swimming – and genetics was one of them. Bjarnason's regime, one that had never been undertaken with a sportsman on the Faroe Islands, was one of the underlining factors, but there was some plausibility in Faroese genetics: the Nordic ancestry, the rowing races between villagers. Those tough Atlantic arms must have come from somewhere.

I was put at ease by Dr Magni Mohr, a senior research fellow at the University of Exeter, who happened to also grow up in a house just fifty metres from Pal's in Vagur.

'I don't believe Pal's success has anything to do with the lifestyle of the Faroese. It is a result of very good coaching and hard work. His maximum oxygen uptake is different compared to other swimmers, as is his low body fat and length of his arms that are needed for him to be successful. A lot of people don't have the capacity to reach that level. In some sense he has inhaled some talents that are related to his genetics.

'But I don't believe it has anything to do with being on the Faroe Islands. It's all down to willpower. In any sport you have to have the genetic potential. In Pal's case he had been born with some possibilities but, again, it is down to the hard work considering the conditions he has been competing against. That's where I have seen Pal as an athlete.

'He has completely changed the way the Faroese perceive sports; that they too can compete at the highest level. Growing up in a place like the Faroes perhaps makes you tougher as people don't complain that much. Anything is possible but I don't think it has anything to do with the way we consume our diet, the rowing we have done over the generations or how many mountains we have walked over because people have been doing the same in different climates.'

Still, Pal's coach was adamant that there was a 'genetic advantage'. His fibre type compositions, he said, seemed to be designed for endurance sports. 'That is also something that is genetically needed. Usain Bolt has a lot of sprint fibres. You need to have that to compete on the world stage.'

Meanwhile, the good doctor said there was still an argument to get up-and-coming Faroese swimmers to train long distance over the shorter, sexier disciplines.

'The fact that the Faroes have this coach who has trained the country's most successful swimmer and that there is an islander who might be genetically disposed to doing 1500 metres? The Faroese are a beguiling, mysterious place. Perhaps it is true.'

For now, Pal wasn't thinking of home and Suduroy. He was in Croatia on his last training camp pre-Olympics. The nerves were beginning to kick in. It was warm – he was also sleeping in an oxygen tent so tried not to go to the bathroom, but he was drinking a lot of water 'so I had to go!' – and Pal had started to think of the Games.

Before his last block of training, Pal did a broken set of 1500m swims, recording twelve or thirteen seconds lower than the world record. He had a low heart rate and looked in fine fettle.

The belief of his coach and the Faroes meant that he was now fighting for gold with the Chinese. 'That was his goal and he was going to surprise people, I was quite sure,' recounts Bjarnason.

'The Faroese thought I was a medal contender,' Pal explains. 'I thought I was and my coach was really sure I was. But when we arrived in London, we talked too much about swimming and didn't take in the experience of the Olympics.'

Pal swam the 400m freestyle on the opening day of the Games at the Aquatics Centre and just missed the final by 0.10 seconds, qualifying ninth.

Or perhaps he might make it... South Korea's Olympic and world champion, Park Tae-Hwan, was sensationally disqualified in his heat following a false start. He had initially come through to overtake the British pacemaker David Carry – who, incidentally, has Faroese roots – and won his heat, only to be denied his place in the final.

But then a reprieve from officials saw Park take his place in the final. A first Olympic final berth for Pal was quickly taken away.

The days passed slowly for Pal as he set himself up for his 1500m tilt. When he had qualified at the Danish Open, Pal was by far the fastest. There was talk of how fast he could now go in the Olympics. Failing to advance through in the 4x200m relay with his Danish teammates hardly helped matters.

Meanwhile, a Faroese TV crew and two radio stations were following his every move on the Olympic Park, though there had been a stumbling block for the small media circus. As they were not accredited by the IOC, they were forced to wait for coach and swimmer to sneak out of the venue so that interviews could be catered for.

'Things are looking good and we haven't prepared for anything other than this, so it better work out,' coach Jon told me before the 1500m heats, when I eventually tracked him down via the Danish team's press officer.

The tactic had been to follow the Chinese 1500m world champion, Sun Yang. But Pal's mind set seemed to be shot as race day approached. Was it walking out in his signature event in Danish colours? Was the Olympic experience just too overpowering?

After 500 metres, Pal was fading fast. Jon, watching just a few metres away on pool deck, and who had noticed Pal's 'special ability' six years previously, was left helpless.

'It was a really dark hour. The whole day was ruined, the whole week was ruined. It was horrible.'

Jon went for a walk after the morning session was over. He kept on walking in the Olympic Park and beyond until he lost his bearings.

'After the 400 metres I got a little bit nervous. He didn't look his best in the latter period of the race. He was struggling, didn't have any rhythm and didn't have the extra strength that he was supposed to have at the end of the race. He took it out like he was supposed to and looked great in the first 200 metres, but there was no closing speed. My suspicions started there. I tried to find out what was going on. We spoke to the Danish team and the team physiologist, who tried to convince Pal that there was nothing wrong, that the training was all there still in his body. What went wrong? There can be so many different explanations.'

So, just what is the feeling like to hit the wall so early in the sport's longest race?

'It gets you and completely the opposite feeling you are striving for. You can't keep your focus on your turns. You feel weak. The last 500 metres were just horrible. Everybody started passing me. When this happens – let alone the middle of the race – then you lose more energy than you imagine. Even though they feel a lot faster, you feel a lot slower.'

The Faroese nation was urging on their man with every stroke back home. However, he finished a disappointing seventeenth overall in 15:18, nearly thirty seconds down on his qualifying mark.

Then came the headlines for the Faroes' first Olympic swimmer: 'Joensen flops horribly in the 1500 metres', 'Olympic dream lasts only 500m'.

Up in the stands sat the small Faroese contingent. 'I was crying at the Olympics,' recalls Prime Minister Johannesen. 'I knew how much he had worked for it. It was a hard blow for me personally, but also for Pal. That moment was one of the hardest moments in sport during these cruel minutes. We could see, feel and hear it that he wasn't going to qualify. We were all crying together, the family, his girlfriend. I invited them all out that night, to speak and get it out of our system and encourage them to come back.'

Then comes a smile, six months after his memory of that day in London. 'But Pal has worked hard to get back to the top and he is doing it already.'

Pal's mother, Thurid Kjaerbo, who had travelled as his physio to international events prior to London, felt her son's pain.

'I can always feel how he is thinking. Is it a good day or bad day? I always knew how he was going to swim before he jumped in the pool. In London, it was so hard. As parents, we don't mind if he is number 1 or number 5, but it was his feelings that we were worried about. There was talk about it before that he could actually be the winner. But really he wasn't ready. He was only a little boy. But it doesn't matter. He wasn't a loser! He was always in front. Perhaps not number 1, but it is what made him continue to swim I think. He should be at his peak in Rio. If he medals in Rio then the doors might open to be a totally independent country.'

In the aftermath came the explanations of his performance. When he started with the Danish team, he had tweaked some techniques, such as a longer stroke. Was his stroke too long? Or perhaps it was inexperience and concentrating on the result, not the process? Perhaps it was that last training block that pushed him over the edge?

Jon says, 'It was very unfortunate that he joined the Danish team when he did. He went from doing much too little, to improving a lot. The Danish team before the Olympics were one of the strongest. When they were capable of training more, they went for more and they were pushed too much. Pal came on to the team and the thing is, you don't need to push Pal, you need to talk him down. In the end, he worked himself into the ground. I'm guessing, but I think this is the most logical explanation for his performance in London.

'It is really rare to motivate him. I never had to say to him to wake up. In the pool, he would kill himself. I would have to slow him down. I think that was part of the problem over the past year. He was just going too fast and doing too much and getting too bulky.'

Jon says that after Pal started training in Copenhagen, in 2011, his body weight shot up to 82 kilograms, whereas in Shanghai, where he went so close to world bronze over 1500 metres, he weighed 73 kilograms. 'That's a big difference for a distance swimmer when you think about oxygen consumption.'

The death of Pal's friend Alex Dale Oen in Arizona was also a pivotal moment. 'That really affected my performance in London. My philosophy had always been that hard work pays off. I kind of lost that after the Olympics.'

His Olympic energy sapped in Stratford, he lost confidence immediately after the Games. He had moved to Denmark, a new culture, colours and coach. Back home he may have been able to drive his car down the hill to the pool in two minutes, but in Copenhagen he had an hour on the bus. It was going to take time to adapt.

'We knew that it was a hard time for him,' says Pal's mother. 'We knew how he felt when he got beat. He was full of regret. What if he didn't choose swimming? What if he chose another lifestyle outside the sport? But he realised it was a part of sport, the losing feeling. It left a mark but you learn as long as you live so…' Her words trail off.

Pal rarely thinks about London now, but it was time for him to take stock, continue his new life in Copenhagen with girlfriend, Malan, and regain that confidence.

The 'Pal Effect' has entered Faroese society, both in business and education

6

THE PAL EFFECT

May 2013, Torshavn. The supporters' cow bells ring out across the packed Torshavn swimming pool, the largest on the islands. Coaches and swimmers cramp the pool deck on one side, while a moving television camera on wheels hogs the other side of the pool.

Members of each island team are willing their teammates on. As soon as he or she turns for breath, they motion forward with their arms, hoping that they might be noticed and it might make all the difference come the finish.

At the far end of the building is a vertical flag of the Faroes, draped from ceiling to floor. The lighting is aquamarine and it makes for a cosy, intimate atmosphere. After all, the 2013 Faroese Short Course Championships are being beamed live across the islands, a stone's throw away from the national football stadium with its newly erected floodlights which look not too dissimilar from four fly swatters.

Throughout the day, all the local television channel had shown was the colour test card and a pre-recorded church service. Now, viewers were witnessing a live one-man show in the form of Pal Joensen, entered into an energy-sapping fifteen events by Suduroy coach Jon Bjarnason, who was looking on intently at his charges from the middle of the pool.

In the 50m men's butterfly, he saw a one-two – a Joensen one-two for that matter – as Pal's younger brother, Eyobjorn, shaded the two-length event.

At the 2008 European Juniors, Eyobjorn had been asked on live radio whether he had expected Pal to win three golds and he replied, 'Yes, I did, because he is also the best in our country.' Five years on, he had beaten his older brother, albeit in an event which Pal was not in full-time training for.

But that's about as good as it got for anyone else during the championships. 'And with a winning time of … PAL JOENSEN' became an over-familiar phrase throughout the two days as he edged ever closer to 100 national championship titles, a record he achieved the following year. One hundred golds! Surely a record in any sport, anywhere for an individual athlete? When a local policewoman handed out the medals for one of the races, it was the first sign of the police I had seen all week.

Later, he was to be interviewed yet again by a local TV reporter, Leivur Frederiksen, but they decided to drop the segment as there had simply been too much Pal. Moments later, his swim had been declared a Faroese record so they took the interview. 'Pal is always so calm,' Frederiksen told me later. 'In that way it was so strange that he didn't perform at the Olympics.'

Here, Pal was medal-laden. And so I wondered where he kept all his medals or, indeed, if there was one that stuck out above all? 'I'd like to say the first one, but I don't know when that was! Perhaps 2004, but I only medalled then. To achieve 100 gold medals is a magical moment and it really sticks out.'

All his medals are back at his parents' home in Suduroy. His hundredth sits proudly in his flat in Copenhagen, along with the world short course and European medals he has gleaned in the last few years.

**

The following day I interviewed Pal away from the poolside for the first time, in a restaurant down by the harbour. Tables were busy, yet Pal wasn't disturbed once throughout the two hours we spent together. Nor did Pal ask why a British journalist had travelled out to write a story about him. I sensed that perhaps he had already thought of the day when media outside his own country would start writing about him, given the mystery of the Faroe Islands.

During the championships, I had sat next to Rokur in the television commentary position as he explained Pal's deep bond with Suduroy. He had travelled back from Copenhagen for the week and was clearly still revelling in swimming for his home town club.

'He was away almost half the year before the Olympics,' Rokur told me. 'Before that, it was Vagur the whole time. He trained there for as long as he could. Training there was a limitation forced upon him because he wasn't offered anything else.'

Now, Pal was describing his rise to becoming a swimming professional over a simple fish dish with boiled potatoes. He took time to digest the questions. He was a thinker, his answers direct.

'Perhaps there is the feeling of being a tough guy and thinking big; the guy who comes from a short course pool, a guy with no strength training, poor facilities in a small country where no one has done anything like it before. I do feel tough and a trend setter in this regard. It has been a big drive for me, a guy out of the ordinary who could do something that nobody has ever done before.

'The drive that made me push myself every single day was to prove that it could be done and that you had to be a tough guy in this environment. If I could do it in these facilities then what could I do in the best facilities? I always felt the underdog. Compared to football, it is a boring sport. Guys and girls swimming back and forth is never going to be a popular thing. We get funding but we certainly can't get money like other sports. Swimming doesn't pass as entertaining here.'

From the moment he hit the water as a junior in Belgrade, this was never going to be a factor for Pal. 'I feel proud of what I have done and achieved. I didn't want to come from a country where people laughed at me and said what a bad swimmer I was.'

Where had he got his mentality from? Was it his father? Kaj Joensen used to be a fisherman with no education. Yet he had worked with little income until he was able to launch his maritime project – and it had paid off.

Kaj had also told me he was, perhaps, a bit 'crazy'. Allan Nielsen, of *Politiken*, had revealed the same. 'The Faroes have their own society in Copenhagen. They have a tradition of being a little bit crazy, but Pal turned out okay! He's not a guy who would do crazy stuff like the Faroese swimming president.'

I asked Jon Hestoy what Nielsen might have been referring to when we met in Barcelona. Thrice a Faroese Swimming Federation President, 1984-85, 1988-96 and 2008 onwards, Hestoy had also been the chief referee of almost every Faroese swimming gala up until 2001. Hestoy, a print publisher by trade, had a profound love for swimming.

I had first seen him on *Trans World Sport*, the global programme which has been an institution for lesser-known sports and sports people, when a TV crew had featured Pal prior to London 2012.

Jon had talked passionately then of the history of swimming on the Faroes and, worryingly, how so few sea fishermen had learnt to swim. But I had never expected Jon to have had such a prodigious career in the pool himself.

According to Jon, the swimming culture in the Faroes was altered thanks to the video revolution in the early seventies.

The Faroes had their first swimming competition in 1912. In Torshavn harbour, festival competitors swam from one pier to the other, where the current government building is situated.

However, it wasn't until Mark Spitz, the great American, raced away with seven gold medals in the pool at the 1972 Munich Olympics that swim-loving Faroese could properly learn the art.

'They had to interpret how Spitz swam. Out here, in a small corner of the world, one stuck in the middle of the Atlantic, enthusiasts could now see the technique. They watched it on film rolls and some improved in the 100 metres by over eight seconds. You can see hardly anything, yet they could see enough. They were trying to do the flip turn, with the help of Super 8 film roll.'

Those 1972 Games sparked a surge of regular swim meetings in late summer after the director of the radio and his son broadcast all the events back home to the Faroes.

Jon's own love affair with the sport began with his old school principal, who was also the swimming coach – except he wasn't a swimmer – as well as being a dab hand at volleyball.

Jon did have a coaching book, *The Science of Swimming* by James 'Doc' Councilman, regarded as one of the greatest coaches and innovators in the sport. He also had a magazine about an old Russian swimmer. 'We tried to figure out how the hell to flip over at the turn from these pages. We had no knowledge of swimming and technique.'

Until the first swimming pool was built in 1959 – the first 25m pool built on the Faroes, but it is now a badminton court – the islanders had to swim in the sea. As a four year old, Hestoy's eyes lit up when a swimming pool opened in 1963, the third to be built on the Faroes.

Hestoy's mother was a pain for all school children in their local village. She used to hunt down children who had missed swim lessons. Girls used to excuse themselves, blaming their period. 'But you had that last week,' would be the response.

Hestoy moved to Denmark in the mid-seventies where he had ambitions of becoming a photographer. Instead he became a printer and joined the local swimming club made famous by Sweden's Suzanne Nilsson, the only western breaststroker who managed to place herself amongst the litany of eastern Europeans from Russia, Bulgaria and Hungary.

As befits Pal's tale, Hestoy was also a distance swimmer who would train three to four kilometres in the morning and twelve kilometres in the evening.

It worked and he won his first medal in 1978, before becoming Danish champion in 1979. He stayed a further three years, until the Faroese garnered their FINA membership and he was able to become the first islander to compete at a World Championships, in Ecuador 1982.

Back then, going abroad to compete for the Faroes was considered an unrealistic prospect. 'But when will you get a proper job?' was a regular thought for most islanders.

Hestoy, now a well-built man as you'd expect from someone who has been out of the competition pool for several decades, is made from different stock. He held seven national records and won eight Danish titles and at one point held the record in 200m butterfly, 400m individual medley and 1500m freestyle. My eyes open. That is quite I spread, I comment. 'Yes, a real man's game,' he says.

In 1982, he took the plunge and moved to southern California and Mission Viejo, the place to be seen if you were a distance swimmer and 'believed' in metres.

He came back after a lean year, but still carved his rivals apart when he returned to Scandinavia thanks to his training regime. Undeterred, he set about entering the *Guinness Book of Records* for the longest swim over 24 hours in a Danish 25m pool.

He had started out his quest at three o'clock in the afternoon after being allowed to leave work early at lunchtime from his printers' job. Four hours later, he had his first and only intake of food, a piece of dark bread, while every half an hour he quenched an energy drink and stopped for around thirty seconds.

He went to the bathroom once and felt in good shape for the first sixteen hours. Thereafter, like the marathon runner who hits that 21-mile mark, was pure hell. He realised he was now in the early throes of morning and at 7am thought to himself that he had a whole working day of swimming left ahead of him. He started hallucinating. As he continued, so he felt as if he was in a dream. 'Dreaming while awake' is how he describes it.

His best friend, Peter S. Agger, was poolside throughout the 24 hours. The pair had erected some speakers used for synchronised swimming in the pool. Jon vividly remembers the soundtrack to the musical *Hair* being repeated endlessly. Especially the lyrics:

Now that I've dropped out, why is life dreary, dreary?
Answer my weary query, Timothy Leary, dearie
Oh, Manchester, England, England across the Atlantic Sea

It wasn't all plain sailing. The record was being attempted just after the official opening of the pool after refurbishment. The pair were promised that the water temperature would be 26.5 degrees Celsius, but it was at least 1.5 degrees below their request and, by the end of his quest, you could see the blood from his joints.

However, he finished 'the job' and even managed to do celebratory butterfly strokes for the last ten metres.

Hestoy clocked up 89,174 metres over 24 hours, just short of ninety kilometres non-stop and equating to an average of around seven kilometres per hour. He was, he admits, 'dead meat' at the end of the record bid, but the celebrations told a different story.

He was greeted with vociferous support all round the pool deck as he was handed a red rose and a bottle of champagne, which he somehow managed to keep above the water surface in his victory lap in the middle of the pool. As he climbed the pool steps, he was surrounded by well-wishers and Danish photographers. Jon couldn't stop smiling.

'The attempt got some really good press in *Jyllands Posten*, the biggest newspaper in Jutland,' Jon recalls. 'The other newspaper in Aarhus, *Aarhus Stiftstidende*, only ridiculed the attempt as their editor hated our coach.'

It took him four days before he could dress himself in the aftermath and, in hindsight, his team could have been more scientific in choosing what foods he consumed. However, this was 1982, not 2012 – no technology and laptops aided Hestoy.

For Jon, the record was 'water under the bridge' and he didn't follow what happened to his world record in the aftermath. 'Looking back, the record ended my career as a swimmer. My pain threshold changed. Before, I did not stop for pain, but after I backed down it started hurting every time.'

In fact, Jon's record lasted for four years when, in 1986, a Michigan swimmer, Dave Goch, attempted to go further over 24 hours. Covered in Vaseline, he had Guinness officials watching every stroke over his 56.8 mile effort, beating Jon's previous mark of 55.41 miles.

What had driven him on to achieve the mark, Goch was asked. 'I had a bad collegiate season and was disappointed in myself. It was very important for me. And it saved the season for me.'

Hestoy has since spent nearly twenty years overseeing Faroese swimming, a job he describes as a basic operation, with just three 25-metre and fifteen small pools on the island.

His biggest mission has been trying to get the Faroese to swim. 'Currently, forty-nine per cent of eleven and twelve year olds can swim. Considering that swimming is part of the school curriculum (one lesson per week), this figure should be above ninety per cent.'

Then there is the problem of local fisherman in the Faroes. 'Fishermen don't die on the high seas, they fall down between the boats in the harbours. Still today, you meet a lot of fishermen who say it is better not to be able to swim.'

For hundreds of years, the Faroese have depended on the sea for industry. The fishing trade has also brought its fair share of sorrow with it, with whole villages wiped out due to drownings. Learning to swim, the fishermen say, merely prolongs the pain of those swept overboard. It is one reason why the Faroese Federation's mission is to get every youth learning to swim, to be on an even par with Iceland, who made it part of legislation.

'The crazy thing', continues Jon, 'is that when the Faroese Federation asked the school children where they had learnt to swim, only a minority said at school. Some said the local club, but most said from their brothers or sisters on vacation. When the Federation goes out to the islands to test their results on how far pupils can swim, the other problem is, for a normal fifth grader, the likelihood of bragging about their ability. So the figures could indeed be worse than forty-nine per cent.'

There is one lady on the Faroes, however, who most islanders should look up to as an inspiration.

Hailing from Vestmanna – a place I'd heard that the farmers are the strongest of all Faroese and who had no problem carrying sheep on their shoulders – an octogenarian has been swimming in the sea every day for over fifty years. Children call her the Swimming Granny.

Born in 1924, she had always swum in the sea and always loved the ocean. She began to swim regularly when she'd had her daughter and fell ill after the birth. 'I didn't eat, I had no energy,' she told her grandson, who produced a well-received short documentary on her life, entitled *Waves: A Portrait of Maria a Heygu*. It's a story less about swimming, more the link between humanity and nature.

'I'd become very thing, terribly thin. I may have weighed less than a hundred pounds, and I lost my milk. And then I didn't have the strength to carry her upstairs. It was then that my husband suggested I started swimming as it was supposed to be good for you.'

And so she did. She regained the will to live and now she is 'so grateful to the ocean'.

'I think the Faroes are so beautiful. Nature is very close to my heart. Always has been. I look out every morning to see what the sea is like. I draw back the curtains to see what the weather is like. The sea draws me closer.'

She eats her porridge, puts on her maroon dressing gown and clogs and walks down to the rocky shore and dives in, no matter what the weather.

On a bad morning she will do forty-five strokes out, and forty-five back. On a good day, she will up her work rate to seventy-five. 'Even if the waves are breaking up the stairs, I go. I'm never afraid of the sea.'

She should be an inspiration, but the Faroese are prone to stick to dry land, perhaps due to the lack of white beaches and warm waters. After all, darkened waters lurk menacingly as soon as you step off shore, while the water is, frankly, freezing.

**

The first time I'd heard the phrase 'the Pal Effect' came when I met the Faroese Prime Minister.

A former football goalkeeper, Johannesen came into parliament in 2002, became Union Party leader two years later and the country's leader in 2008. 'Just when the world crisis came in,' he laughs. 'I am lucky I have been experiencing a lot since then! Just like in sports, just when things are going against you, you learn the most. Small is beautiful, big is powerful in different aspects of life. But Europe is our main market for all our industry. And we are totally dependent on the world outside. We export ninety-eight per cent [unsurprisingly, fish is the main export volume] and import the same. We are together with Denmark. We have a political system which is second to none. We do our fishery agreements with Norway and Russia for example, and not going to the European Union in Brussels in that respect.

'We are a stable environment, have a flexible workforce and everything we do in our culture is about the sea water. We have been losing so many fishermen at sea. If you go back fifty years, no one could really swim. We lost so many people in the fjords and narrow waters when they were rowing, as they were not able to swim.

'So now that we have one of the world's best swimmers, water is connected to our history. Without Pal in the Faroes, we have been average in swimming. He means so much to the Faroese people. He gives out this courage in competition and he is a character that brings people together. The mentality he brings in is tremendous.

'I once asked a young guy who was twelve or so about swimming, and he said that one day he would like to defeat Pal. Before that, he wanted to defeat all the stars out in the big world. So now the youngsters are trying to compete up to Pal. He is creating a new mentality with his hard work, considering he trains up to thirty-five hours per week. After all, the footballers only train less than half of that. Swimming has put new emphasis on how much you need to work to succeed – not only on the islands but the international scene.'

I'd heard Johannesen describe Pal as 'a lighthouse' before and, here he was saying it again in his well-appointed, bright government building.

He recognised Pal as this beacon when he'd put a gold medal around Pal's neck at a previous Island Games. The Faroese were going to need a 50m swimming pool now. 'No, no,' said a Swedish swimming coach. 'We need to go down to 25m pools after what he has achieved!'

'Pal is more than a swimmer in the Faroes,' the Prime Minister says. 'He is a national role model for the youths here. In all different aspects of society, be it trade, politics or business, they are looking to this guy who has said he wants to be a world champion since an early age. The Pal Effect.

'Nobody has thought about that before, an island in the middle of nowhere and here the youths are saying that they will be champions of Faroe Islands. But Pal has always been speaking that he can beat everybody. The goals he has been setting are ones most people dream about. Pal sees it as a reality. In a small society, where people are very close, we have made a thing about people thinking they are *something*. We should work on the opposite actually and that is what Pal is striving for.'

The sense I got from my time on the islands was that Pal's success didn't just have an impact on sports. To have a national hero was beneficial for any nation trying to build, in all facets of society.

'All people like to be identified towards a winner, yet there is no arrogance in Pal,' the Prime Minister agreed. 'There is not an ounce of that in him. So it is easy to love such a character.'

A character who has yet to experience the Olympic dream of competing under his own flag.

'We applied to the IOC in the eighties and they changed the rules in 1986 where they said that sovereign countries could only be included. But we had applied before that so we are asking the committee for fair play as they changed the charter. We never had a real answer to us and that is what we are working towards.'

Twenty years after their original application, in January 2004, the Faroese Confederation of Sports and Olympic Committee sent another letter to the IOC concerning the restatement of application for Olympic recognition.

Enclosed with the submission were letters of support from the Danish and Faroe Prime Ministers at the time. Edited extracts from the letter included the following:

The Faroe Islands are in a quite similar situation to that of Aruba, Cayman Islands and the Cook Islands that were recognised in the 1980s at the same time as the Faroese application was processed. In all, thirteen National Olympic Committees are recognised without being fully independent.

The Faroe Islands submitted its application for Olympic recognition in 1984. In our view this is the relevant application date, since that date several National Olympic Committees representing comparable countries have been recognised.

It is primarily because the Faroe Islands are already recognised by almost all relevant International Sports Organisations that we seek Olympic Recognitions as the Crowning Achievement and a necessity for further strengthening of international ties.

Our greatest triumph to date was the Paralympic recognition of the Federation of Faroese Athletes with Disabilities our participation in the Paralympics under Faroese National Flag, winning a number of medals, from Seoul 1988 through to Sydney 2000.

And so the letter went on, as did the subsequent wait. A decade later, the current Prime Minister states that, 'there is nothing hindering us from becoming a full member of the IOC. As a former national player, to be allowed to represent our sports people is very important.'

However, in May 2015, a breakthrough – and history – was made when Johannesen and the IOC president, Thomas Bach, met for the first time to discuss the issue of the Faroe Islands becoming an independent Olympic member.

'Of course, it would be my greatest goal as a Prime Minister if Pal could represent the Faroese flag at the Olympics. We are working towards that through lobbying. There is the possibility of going into the Games with our flag and this is our dream. I had the privilege of doing this in football as we are a full member of FIFA.'

For a man who has overseen Pal's rise from the highest step in Faroese swimming, Jon Hestoy is adamant that the country's greatest sporting asset should also be well catered for when he retires, as an Olympian or otherwise. Since 2009, the Faroese Swimming Federation has received a healthy grant from the government for Pal's preparations. 'If he was an artist on that level, he would receive a lifelong allowance from the government. One day he will quit but somehow a nation must give this guy some kind of lifelong achievement. He can't just be the greatest Faroese sportsman in our history and everyone says "goodbye" and that's it. So that will be a challenge when we reach that point. He is an intelligent guy and he is still learning how to swim his races. His maturity will change his way of competing, I'm sure of that.'

And if the day ever came, the day when the IOC give the Faroes the green light, there could only ever be one choice as flag bearer, one leading out the small Faroese contingent, nestled between Ethiopia and Fiji in the greatest sporting show on earth.

The Faroese contingent at the 2013 World
Championships in Barcelona

7

THE FAROES AND THE WORLDS

The Palau Sant Jordi arena sits atop Montjuic, the broad hill overlooking Barcelona, and stands next to the Olympic Stadium, renovated for the Barcelona Games in 1992. These were the Games that famously saw Paralympic archer Antonio Rebollo light the Olympic flame via an arrow.

With billions watching on television, his accuracy looked to be spot on until it later emerged that effects specialist Reyes Abades had actually lit the cauldron via remote control. Still, Barcelona set a benchmark with that opening ceremony.

On the track, who could forget those still vivid, emotional scenes when British 400m runner Derek Redmond had to be helped across the line by his father after he tore a hamstring.

The swimming back in 1992 actually took place at the nearby Piscines Bernat Picornell, a 50m outdoor venue. It was a pity, then, that the swimming World Championships took place indoors. There's nothing like an open air press box.

Considering the modern way of presenting events these days, however, it made sense for FINA to go indoors. The slick lighting, plus the enclosed atmosphere gave more theatre and edge to proceedings.

None more so than when there was a world record, the four screens high above flashing 'WORLD RECORD!' for several minutes, while another camera caught a volunteer with a huge FINA flag with 'WORLD RECORD' emblazoned on it.

All we really wanted to see were the faces on the world record holders, but by the time all the hoopla had stopped and the event presentation crew had stopped fanning themselves in their studio, the swimmers had all but surfaced onto the pool deck, retrieved their lanyards and were off doing an interview for television.

The weather during the championships touched thirty degrees Celsius throughout, meaning that indoors was a trifle humid. However, the atmosphere replicated that of the Aquatics Centre at London 2012. There was a smattering of British support at each session. Croats, Germans and Italians were here too. Of course, the Spanish whooped and hollered with every entrance of one of their own.

But it was the French who stole the show. There were hundreds of them, no doubt still celebrating the seven medals they mustered in London. The Tricolore was everywhere, too. The French support was rewarded with success, which seemed to galvanise the squad.

There was near pandemonium when Olympic champion Yannick Agnel won the 200m men's freestyle on the third night of racing. What a lovely gentleman. And what a battle back to the top of the podium. After leaving his long-time coach, the Frenchman took the plunge and travelled to Baltimore after the Olympics where the great Bob Bowman, who led Phelps to so many Olympic golds, took him under his wing.

Chatting to his rivals after they hauled themselves from the pool, bantering with the Russian Danila Izotov, who won bronze, Agnel was, you could say, delighted. And the crowd revelled in every hand wave that came their way from the man who first came on to the scene as a seventeen year old at the same European Championships, in Budapest, where Pal won silver in 2010.

'This is as beautiful as London,' said Agnel, who waved to his support at every opportunity, his smile as wide as the Montjuic. He then spent an eternity with the beautiful presenters of Eurosport.

The Faroese sent four swimmers for the 2013 Championships. Pal, of course, plus three others, two of whom broke national records. Pal had now changed coaches from Paulus Wildeboer to Shannon Rollason, the Australian, with the former having left to head up Queensland Swimming.

Wildeboer was Pal's first coach when he moved to Denmark and still kept in touch with training schedules for the period when there was no head coach after the former's departure.

Before he left, Pal had arranged to attend a training camp in Australia with Denis Cotterell, a legend of long-distance coaching. When he arrived in Brisbane, Pal still hadn't heard from him. After the two weeks were up, he wrote an email and a reply came back with the shocking news that he had been diagnosed with prostate cancer.

Thus it was that a day before Pal left Australia, Wilde-boer travelled to Brisbane and was soon to learn that it was likely to be their last meeting.

He kept on writing to Pal, telling him how well the treatment was going. But contact soon faded as he couldn't find the energy to write emails and almost a year later, in May 2014, he died. 'He was a very optimistic guy. He always talked to us on what you put in, you get back…'

**

If London saw the emergence of American star swimmer, sixteen-year-old Katie Ledecky, then Barcelona confirmed that this outstanding teenager wasn't just a one-off and could back up her performances by banking gold and world records.

The American let down the London 2012 party at the Aquatics Centre by blistering out of the starting blocks in the 800m freestyle final, which proved a trying experience for eventual bronze medallist Rebecca Adlington.

A year on and Ledecky's grounded talent shone through again in the 1500 metres, surging ahead on the final turn to win world gold. Lotte Friis of Denmark and a Kiwi swimmer all dipped under world record pace too. But Ledecky it was who banked her second gold after winning the 400m freestyle on the opening night.

Friis is something of a star in Denmark. In 2009, she appeared on the Danish version of *Strictly Come Dancing – Vild med Dans –* and is a hot property for the tabloids in Copenhagen. Moreover, she has trained with Joensen at camps and her silver must have given a huge boost to Joensen ahead of his final the following evening.

The distance events are obviously a far cry from the frenetic turns of the splash and dash. Even more so when you consider the 50m butterfly; Mark Foster, the former British sprint swimmer, once told Eurosport viewers 'there are pianos crashing everywhere!' during the 2010 Europeans, presumably in reference to hands going into a whirling overload, like a Rachmaninov piece.

The 800m freestyle and beyond were still utterly compelling races to watch. Even more so down in the mixed zone afterwards, where it was evident that Ledecky and Friis were barely out of breath in speaking to the media. One must also wonder, with Ledecky's success in the 1500 metres, whether American TV executives would actually hold out for a mere fifteen minutes before cutting to a commercial.

The viewers would have missed out. For it was neck and neck all the way, stroke for stroke inside world record pace, until the final 150 metres. From here on in, the sixteen year old romped to a world record (15:36.53), smashing the previous mark by over six seconds. Put simply, this powerhouse schoolgirl can swim a mile faster than some people can run it.

Meanwhile, there was a worry as to how Pal might perform in the Catalan capital. His qualifying time in the 800 metres, 8:03.70, was some eighteen seconds slower than the time set by China's Sun Yang.

However, a few months before the championships, Pal had visited Cotterell on the Gold Coast at a time when the rainy season was in full effect in the Faroe Islands. The training camp, with its two Olympic-sized pools, was to be another string to Pal's bow as he looked to gain ground in long distance disciplines heaped with burgeoning talent.

Cotterell, a master coach since undertaking his first session in 1967, is renowned for taking Australian national icon Grant Hackett to gold in the 1500 metres at both the 2000 and 2004 Olympics. More recently, he coached Sun Yang to London 2012 gold, but was to soon cut ties with the Chinese.

A tough, dedicated coach, Cotterell also used to hand out 1000m butterfly sets for misbehaving young charges, though he never made them finish the punishment. 'I can say that I've never met anyone like him. He's one of a kind,' Olympian Giaan Rooney once noted of Cotterell. 'He'll die with chlorine coming out of his pores. He's an absolute legend.'

At the British trials in Sheffield for the Barcelona World Championships, I met Kevin Renshaw, a British Swimming coach, who waxed lyrical over Cotterell.

'If I look out there at the big wide world for someone to give me ideas, I look at what Denis Cotterell has achieved. He is the only man to coach four swimmers who have swum under fifteen minutes, which is a good benchmark for good distance swimmers. Denis is without doubt the leading person and one of the most passionate coaches I have come across.

'He's an absolute whirlwind when he's on deck. He's volatile as well, has a great knowledge to what it takes and is a great innovator. I spoke to him a few years ago and he said that he had tried everything new that had come along. Now it was "what I know works" not what someone is doing somewhere else.'

The programme Pal ingested during his time on the Gold Coast incorporated the Cotterell work ethic. It is not regarded as a high-volume programme. He has a tough mix of setting out pieces of work with short amounts of rest and extreme high speed. It is far removed from the stereotypical swimming in the seventies and eighties where it was long distance followed by a short rest, over and over.

'Swimmers have gone out to Denis, but with some it doesn't do them much good, because it is such a shift from what they do in their own programmes. They just get beat up! I have people who have come into my programme and they haven't made much progress, because they aren't used to it.'

As talk turned to Pal, Renshaw admitted that the Faroese's early hardships in an inadequate pool could be found elsewhere across the globe, too.

'There are hundreds of programmes pretty similar to that. David Davies [a long distance specialist from Wales] was like that until 2004 when he won his Olympic bronze medal with Dave Haller. He swam at Sophia Gardens at the Welsh Institute of Sport in a four-lane 25m pool. He would go to training camps and get exposure to 50m swimming but Cardiff didn't get its 50m pool until 2008. Daniel Fogg [a British distance swimmer] didn't move to Loughborough until he was nineteen and the only time he set foot in a 50m pool was to race. So there are a lot of people who've had the same journey. But in Australia, they're different. They have produced more teenage wonder kids perhaps, along with the US, who have a massive prevalence towards long course pools.'

In Barcelona, Fogg had reached the 800 metres final but missed out on a 1500 metres berth in a final loaded with talent.

Introduced second to the masses, out came Pal in his traditional blue Faroes' tracksuit. His national flag was now prominent at major championships and Barcelona was no different. With Pal facing the blocks from the side, as he likes to do, he might have seen the Faroese flags being waved directly in front of him from the stands, where his parents were sitting.

One by one they came out, including Ryan Cochrane, the Canadian who had won a medal in this race at the last two World Championships. A third medal was there for the taking, which would have equalled Hackett's record in the discipline.

Enter Sun Yang. A towering, almost basketballer-like figure, decked out in his all white tracksuit and statement headphones.

Sun was last to get down to the blocks, there was an ordered hush from the stadium announcer, and they were away.

From lane seven, Pal could see that the Chinese and the Australian, Jordan Harrison, had fast starts. At the first turn, Pal was seventh. He admitted afterwards that he felt good, his technique was spot on, but his pace wasn't there. Turn by turn, the Faroe was losing touch with the leaders.

This race always belonged to Sun. He was toying with his rivals and if there was a street corner betting syndicate somewhere in Asia laying serious money on when this supremely gifted athlete was going to pull away from the rest, then the odds would have been exceedingly low on the final fifty metres.

For that's all Sun needed to do really. And he duly finished 2.24 seconds ahead of surprise silver medallist Michael McBroom. Cochrane took bronze. And Pal? Well, he finished seventh, a shade over eleven seconds behind Sun.

Afterwards, he seemed to spend an age with Danish TV in the mixed zone, that gracious smile appearing on camera.

Further down the line was a lone British journalist waiting for the Faroes' top athlete. A slightly bizarre experience, I had sometimes thought. But I wanted to get the athlete's thoughts and race summary. How did he feel after that? Was he happy? Any sound bite. It's not a place to get a roots and all exposé on Faroese life, how this swimmer was now a top ten distance racer at world level. It was the here and now.

'On the first 200 metres I saw Sun go for it,' Pal admitted. 'I thought not to put too much speed at the beginning but I really should have gone out a bit quicker.'

Nevertheless, a look down the final start list revealed that Pal was the second-best European at 1500 metres. In the semi-finals, Pal had been the fastest European. But this is a young man's sport now and, sure enough, a tough eighteen-year-old Italian, Gregorio Paltrinieri, snatched sixth place, 2.28 seconds ahead of Pal. In the scheme of things, the stalls had already been set for the 2014 European Championships in Berlin.

Moreover, these championships had changed the views of journalists, commentators and event co-ordinators. No longer was the Faroese flag missing. No longer were questions being asked of how Pal had made the grade from small training pool to 50m world finals.

Or as *Politiken*, the Danish national broadsheet which has called Pal the 'all-time greatest Faroese sporting name', put it: 'As Pal Joensen found at the European Championships in Budapest in 2010, the first time at a major swimming championships, there stood journalists [as I recall, it was just me] queuing up to hear about how you could win medals by training on windswept islands between birds' nests and in a country not renowned for its swimming tradition.'

Pal may have a tale, but Sun Yang's dominance is equally riveting. Without delving too much into the stereotypical Chinese athlete, Sun turned eyes in Barcelona with his public outpouring of emotion after winning his first gold here. He splashed the water and punched the air like Emilio Estevez might have done in *The Breakfast Club*, if he had been sent for detention in the pool, instead of the school library.

Sun had a brilliant London 2012, picking up Olympic golds and world records. But life seemed to unravel thereafter. He was detained for a week after the Porsche he was driving without a license collided with a bus. Then came a row with Sun's coach over a love affair with an air hostess. Sun rejected coach Zhu Zhigen's calls that he stop the relationship and concentrate on his swimming instead.

'Athletes want to get good results, and to do this you need systematic and scientific training without outside interference,' Sun wrote, unusually for a Chinese athlete, on his microblog.

He made the copy coming out of China all the more interesting. A year later, however, came damning repercussions for the swimming sensation. In November 2014, it was revealed that Sun had served a three-month doping ban before being able to return to competition.

At the time, a cover-up was denied by Chinese officials, saying the suspension was unusually short because the then 22-year-old had convinced them that he did not mean to take trimetazidine, a banned stimulant which had been added to the prohibited list that January.

Sun admitted that he'd taken the prescription drug, Vasorel, for heart palpitations since 2008 and was unaware that it contained trimetazidine, which increases blood flow into the coronary arteries.

Some twenty-odd centimetres taller than Pal, Sun's style means that he is often seen to be gliding in comparison to his rivals, a clear advantage being forged – if he was in shape – thanks to his height.

'We know that he's working hard with every stroke but we also know that he was using a medication to be able to do all this stuff,' says Bjarnason. 'He's admitted since 2008 that he's been using a medicine for a heart condition. He's admitted stupidly enough that he's been using it and there are experts who are totally outraged that he's even able to swim anymore and that his records aren't scratched. What he's done at the Olympics means nothing to me. He's truly a nobody in my book, for everything he's achieved, and there's no respect there. Whether he did it deliberately or by mistake, I don't know. I refuse to believe that a coach of a swimmer that good is so ignorant that they didn't know it was illegal.'

Jon read intensively on the subject in the weeks after the Sun news hit the international media. In the back of his mind, he knew that Pal's fourth place at the World Championships in 2011 could have been so much more, perhaps signifying the Faroes' greatest triumph.

Pal came into that 800 metres final in Shanghai as the second-fastest swimmer. 'What ruined the final for Pal that day was the way Sun Yang swam the medal race. He should never have been in that race and if that was the case, then things could have turned out very differently and we could be looking at a gold medallist. We'll never know.'

After his 800 metres win in Barcelona, two years' on, Sun couldn't control his emotions on the top podium and covered his eyes with his arms as he let go once more. Two down, one to go. With a two-day rest, Sun and Pal would be back for the 1500 metres heats, the former knowing that one more gold in the bag and he would become the male star of Barcelona.

Pal was in an outside lane again and Jon Hestoy had his hands to his mouth and was ringing out Pal's name at the top of his voice before the off.

He was standing, binoculars in hand, alongside a small band of ten Faroese supporters high up in the Palau Sant Jordi. Rokur was standing several blocks along, videoing proceedings. They knew, after the 800 metres, that this was his shot.

Pal was fifth at 100 metres, but leading at 400 metres. On his tail was Cochrane. There were swimmers spread out all over the pool by this point. An Ecuadorian and Egyptian were beginning to feel the pace, while a Chinese and Slovakian were half a pool's length behind either side of Pal.

This was all going rather well and Pal was third at the 1000-metre turn, some four seconds down on Cochrane. At the bell, the Faroese upped their noise levels from the stands. Pal was closing in on the Aussie Jordan Harrison, while Britain's Dann Fogg was also impressing in fourth.

Pal eventually touched in 14:57.76 and after the times had been collated, the Faroese had qualified in fifth for the final. The swim told a story though. After letting his rivals get ahead in the 800 metres, Pal assessed the situation in the 1500 metres heats, didn't get stressed and swam a mature race.

It was clear that life was beginning to become more settled in Denmark.

There were, though, still the odd teething problems that came with swimming – or in this case training – with another country. Denmark's head coach, the Briton Nick Juba, and Pal were at one point hunched over a map of Barcelona and trying to work out how he could get from the Faroese hotel to train with the Danes. The crux of the problem was that the Danes' hotel was another bus line, so Pal ended up taking taxis.

A small problem in the scheme of things. However, ground was being gained under his new coach Rollason, as well as Juba, an easy-going character inside the camp.

With Britain's championships not amounting to much, speaking to Juba shed light on two areas: his thoughts on British swimming and, of course, working with Pal. 'He is learning about his abilities and how to relax more,' Juba said. 'He is terrific, he is a fairy tale story and he is a huge talent, that's for sure. I am sad he can't swim for Denmark more!'

Juba had joined the Danes only a few months prior to Barcelona after being interviewed as one of two candidates for the vacant British head coaching role, a position filled by Bill Furniss, Adlington's former coach.

The sixty-year-old was thrilled at Denmark's success, especially as they had only sent four female swimmers to Barcelona. Not out of his doing, but his predecessor's tough stance on qualifying standards for the worlds.

There was Rikke Moller Pedersen, who produced an outstanding display in her 200m breaststroke semi-final as a Dane broke a world record for the first time since 1959. Then came Friis, who came away with two silvers following a brace of outstanding swims in the 800 metres and 1500 metres.

Juba called the clash between Ledecky and Friis – Britain's Jazz Carlin failed to qualify despite being world number 1 heading into the event – as one of the 'best races he'd ever seen'. He did, though, admit that he got Friis's tactics wrong as the American swam away on the final length of a searing final.

Ledecky wrapped up her meet with a fourth gold medal and second world record in her 800 metres win. And just to rub salt into the wounds of British Swimming, Ledecky then went under Adlington's world record.

Such is Ledecky's character, she then handed the flowers from the medal podium to Adlington, via the BBC interviewer, Sharron Davies. The youngster left Barcelona saying that she hoped to pass her driving test when she got home. Swimming is such an easy game.

Joensen was not the only Faroe swimming on the final day. Hestoy's son, Bartal, was also competing in the 400 metres individual medley. His personal best of 4:36.32 was some thirty seconds behind Phelps' staggering world record in the 400 metres. Then again, most of the competitors' qualifying times were not even close to the great American. The same applied to Sun, the Haile Gebrselassie of distance swimming.

So, to the final individual race of the eight-day championships: the 1500 metres. Back in the Faroes, the modern digital age had finally clocked on. By all accounts, Pal's fourteen or so minutes in the water was going to be the first ever live blog published on any subject on the internet.

The eight swimmers came out and in a shot they were up on to the blocks and away, Pal with a wave to his support up in the stands.

The Faroese was actually first away out of the blocks into his first stroke, but that's about as good as it got. He slowly slipped down the field. Sun and Cochrane were neck and neck at 750 metres and then again at 1400 metres.

Sun's languid strokes suggested he was in yet another comfort zone. The way he operates through his stroke is akin to sliding on ice with no arm movement. It is that fluid. And he seemed to be toying with the field here. Pal, meanwhile, admitted afterwards that he felt early on he couldn't keep up with the leaders and swam his own race.

Sun wasn't exactly doing the same. After twenty-eight laps, the Canadian was still on Sun's shoulders. But with two laps to go, Sun upped the gears and raced to another gold. Paltrinieri, the in-form Italian, snatched bronze.

Pal finished eighteen seconds off bronze, but it meant that he was still the second-best European in the world over the longest distance in swimming. The Faroese contingent was happy with the performance and it all pointed towards more success in Berlin and the 2013 European Championships. Could he finally convert silver to gold?

What was abundantly clear too was that Pal wasn't 'the joke of the meet anymore', as one Nordic journalist told me.

Allan Nielsen, of Danish daily *Politiken*, had covered seven Olympics as the paper's swimming correspondent and admitted that Pal 'had been taken seriously and he deserves it'.

'It was a funny story initially at the European Championships in Budapest,' he explained before one evening session in Barcelona. 'The Faroese have a self-understanding that is enormous. Every time I write a story about Pal I get much more reaction to his stories than anything else. They are really keen about mistakes. The first time I wrote anything about Pal was at the European Juniors in 2008 where he had a battle with a Dane, Anders Lie Nielsen. I might have said something wrong about the times and I received about six emails explaining the fact. That's how they are up there.

'If he was to qualify for the team, it became a little bit particular as they fought for that one place. At the start he was considered a loner. Could he connect and become part of the Danish squad? But that happened easily and he quickly became an established member of the team.

'When I first heard about this story, the first reaction was that they ate all this funny stuff up there. But it wasn't that exotic! Pal is just a calm, nice guy. He has adapted so well. To the Danes, the Faroes will always be a part of Denmark, just as Greenland is. It's more the other way around, the Faroes find it very hard to except that he has to swim under the Danish flag.'

For all the perceptions that Denmark is a swimming nation, Nielsen says that swimming is not a big sport. He was the only reporter who covered the 2005 World Championships, while swimming disappeared in the media until Friis became the first Danish world champion in 2009. It is still behind football, handball, speedway, badminton and golf.

It feels that way in England, too. Despite numbers falling, 2.6 million adults took part in a weekly swimming session during 2014, making it the highest participation sport in England. Yet, only four British journalists saw Adam Peaty break a world record and show his thrusting muscles to the world in Berlin at the European Championships in 2014.

Anyway, an hour after speaking to Nielsen, Pedersen rolled up for her 200m women's breaststroke semi-final, swam 2:19.11, and set a world record.

Catching international attention – German media
interview Pal in Berlin

8

FROM BUDAPEST TO BERLIN

British journalists' knowledge of open water swimming had slowly increased thanks to the efforts of Keri-Anne Payne in the gruelling, lonely art of 10km races, the marathon of swimming.

After finishing a dreaded fourth in the 800m women's freestyle at the 2006 Commonwealth Games in Melbourne, Payne assessed her career and attempted to try out distance swimming, given that it was to be a new event at the 2008 Olympics.

At her first World Championships, only her second ever swim, she noticed some unwanted invaders close to the swimmers during a warm-up swim: jellyfish 'the size of dinner plates' as she sprinted in the opposite direction. She has swum next to shark nets, encountered dead dogs and horses' heads, but still became a world champion.

Self-navigation is crucial over the two hours it roughly takes for the women to finish the course. Even looking up to check your direction takes time and can lose you energy. Then comes the trickery of getting one over your rival – it's not uncommon to be pushed underwater by fellow competitors' arms – hence the officials' motor boats, complete with red and yellow cards for misdemeanours.

Pal had first encountered open water swimming when he raced at the Great London Swim in 2010, finishing a credible fourth after the sixteen minutes he spent in the Docklands water.

That same year he had travelled to what he describes as 'battle camps', with all the long distance swimmers in Potsdam, Germany. Pal and co had been invited to train together for two weeks and 'beat the hell out of each other'. With so many long-distance athletes meeting up, it was a different experience for Pal, who was more in tune with training alone at his own pace.

'It was the sort of swimming I needed to be doing. I realised I couldn't focus on the 400 metres and the 1500 metres. The original plan was to do the 1500 metres and the 10 kilometres at the Olympics.'

So, following his London 2012 exertions, he took three weeks off and started training for one week for the European Championships in Tuscany. For his first ever 5 kilometres and 10 kilometres, it was, he says, a fun experience, finishing tenth and 'way back' respectively.

The Danish coaches were confident that Pal could be a medal candidate in the open water due to the way he trained: he had completed several 5km time trials to keep his endurance at a high level and had felt a good sense of satisfaction in doing so. Not many people can admit to that.

He realised, however, that he had to gain experience in navigation and swimming as a group. Excitement was building as he landed in Berlin for the open water events – traditionally held the week before the pool events – prior to his signature events the following week.

Pal also knew that he lacked the armoury for and experience of a long distance event. But he knew that he was as fast as the more experienced swimmers and could post a medal time.

'I always get a bit nervous when he does open water swimming,' says Malan, Pal's then fiancée. 'There is no history of open water swimming in the Faroes. It's just too cold and not even practical wearing a wetsuit.'

In open water there is a countdown from ten, the first signal. From five seconds, there is a beep, then a long beep and off they go. There can sometimes be a difference of one second between the medals at the end of a two-hour race, but who wants to false start in such a gruelling race anyway?

In Berlin, Pal had started counting from four seconds himself. Four-three-two-one… and off he dived.

Suddenly, he realised that he'd maybe heard the long beep after his entry into the water. He should have really counted from five. He didn't know that the last beep was a different, longer one.

There was no time to think – Pal was away. He swam for around 500 metres before the eagle-eyed officials started to near the lead group. At first, Pal thought they were swimming off course. But then they held out Pal's race number, so he took his head out of the water to communicate with the officials' boat.

False start, they said. Disbelief.

'I was really pissed. I knew that I was in good enough shape to be in the medal count. The start signal was not how I expected. In hindsight I should have been more relaxed. When I came in, I watched the race and saw the experienced guys come in. There's nothing I could do it about it. I didn't just come here for medals, I came here to gain open water experience. And the only thing I experienced was a false start – and not to do one again!'

There was a smile from Pal, but I could tell he was far from enamoured by the experience. 'A lot of people have asked me how it came to be and I honestly still can't find a good answer for it.'

Faroese heroism came to my mind, but I didn't want to tell Pal that. 'A lot of swimmers and coaches heard about it. I felt like a celebrity in some way. So many people were talking about it in the swimming environment.'

Eight years previously, Jon Bjarnason had taken Pal to Melbourne so that he could get used to the starting blocks at a major meet. Coach had entered charge into every single freestyle event, though Pal could never understand why.

He was there to seize the moment in Melbourne and not let nerves get the better of him. So when the false start story is relayed to Jon, he says, 'That was not nerves – that was not knowing the rules! The starting procedures are quite different to that of the pool. He just misjudged the timing and I was laughing all week about that one.'

Pal goes on. 'Well, at least I know people were getting excited about me in some way. But to be remembered for this, it was something I was going to have to change. I was always going to be known as the guy who false started in the 5 kilometres the first time he did it at a European Championships! You just have to roll with the punches I guess. I'm just sad that I didn't have a good response to all the jokes levelled at me!'

It was all about self-defence mode after his open water exertions: how to hold more energy for the pool housed inside Berlin's velodrome and how to go one better than his European silver during that sultry day on Margaret Island in Budapest.

'I felt really good in practice. As far as my tapering was concerned, it is a really complicated process to go through. You can't really evaluate it as so many good days and bad days come and go in a taper. Some days you are really hitting the pace times and the next three days you can't even swim a 1500 metres pace.'

I had first come across 'tapering' in Budapest. Despite eighteen medals at those European Championships, most of Britain's swimmers were not race-ready in Hungary, with the main focus on the Commonwealth Games in Delhi.

For the competing Brits, all the talk was about being 'shaved and tapered', meaning that they are fully rested and ready for a major meet.

Liam Tancock, a former world champion backstroker and thoroughly likeable competitor, had visible body hair in Budapest – a sure sign that he was still coming off heavy training. Then, in Delhi, he'd had facial hair in the build-up to the meet, but come the night before his opening heats, he was ready to get the razor out.

I attempted to unravel the phrase for the *Daily Telegraph* and the piece was one of the most read on the whole website. This was a surprise given that the Games had got off to a less than memorable start, and was copy delight for the media.

In the build up and for the opening few days, the *Telegraph* soon had a daily 'what's gone wrong in Delhi today' panel which we were expected to fill with yarns about snakes in the athletes' village, latest dengue fever alerts and half-finished stadiums.

Thankfully, my lack of knowledge on shaving and tapering was backed up by Tancock. 'I don't think anyone truly understands the term unless you know the sport, but it makes so much difference. I had one week's rest in Budapest where usually I would have four weeks. A taper is over three-four weeks where you are getting ready to race fast and you gradually slow down training. The finishing touches to that are the shaving of the body hair and feeling smooth diving into water the night before my first heat of a major championship. The change in feeling is phenomenal and it makes all the difference.'

English Institute of Sport (EIS) practitioners work closely with the British Swimming programme to determine strategies to best prepare athletes to perform in the build up to these major championships.

'We learn from every competition for each athlete as to whether a strategy has worked well or not,' said Ben Holliss, then working for the EIS. 'Swimming is generally a high volume sport, meaning the athletes put in a great deal of training, so tapering regularly is not possible, and as such we typically wouldn't taper down more than two to three times a year. There are a number of things to look at; rest and recovery, travel, body composition and performance data to analyse their preparations in more detail. Tapers are highly event specific. A distance swimmer for example may cut their volume of training but would still be doing a lot compared to a sprinter, who would drop down much more volume and do higher intensity land work.'

Timing when and how athletes taper down their training still requires a combination of data and experience.

'Getting the taper right for athletes is a balancing act; they need to unload enough to feel fresh but not enough to lose their fitness,' according to Barry Shillabeer, former EIS strength and conditioning coach. 'We track each session to see how fresh athletes are and have a certain range for each individual athlete which helps us know if they are going in the right direction. We also keep a lot of data from the past cycle, so we understand where they are. Not only do sports have unique traits in relation to training load and tapering to allow athletes to peak in time for competitions, but individual disciplines and athletes have their own performance demands and responses to training, which require a tailored approach.'

So, with shaving more about the feel of entering the water than anything to do with hydrodynamics, those 'good and bad days' were about to effect Pal, admitting that after the distance events 'it felt good in the water until the day of the 1500 metres heats in the pool'.

Pal – at twenty-three he was the oldest swimmer in the field – was starting inside two Britons, Stephen Milne and Jay Lelliott, a nineteen year old who had survived two operations for a recurrent brain tumour as a child and who, the previous evening, had won a surprise bronze in the men's 400m freestyle on the opening night.

Six were in a line at the 500-metre mark. Italian Gabriele Detti the early front runner, a stroke ahead of Pal. At the halfway mark, Detti had eked out a one second lead, but with Pal's stroke pattern looking in good nick.

At 800 metres, Detti stole a turn and opened up a three-length gap as Pal started to go backwards. I had met Rokur in the press centre before the race and, after his open water experiences, he didn't want to have to explain why Pal had failed again in his strongest discipline.

With 300 metres left, Milne and Lelliott had taken hold of second and third, with a Slovak edging ahead of Pal. This really wasn't going to plan.

'I just couldn't hit the pace. I was going well for the first 500 metres but when I tried to progress and take the lead I just didn't feel comfortable. Swimmers started passing me and I got really tired.'

But the saving grace was that this heat was going at a fair old lick. When the Italian touched first, the chasing quarter weren't far behind. When Pal touched in fifth, clocking 15:08.02, he was in danger of missing out on the final altogether.

He had recorded a quicker time than the winner of the opening heat, so to be assured of a final berth, no more than three swimmers had to be faster in the final heat. Defending champion, the Italian speedster Paltrinieri, who had finished as the leading European ahead of Pal in the 1500 metres world final, was a locked on favourite to advance. So too, Gergely Gyurta, the Hungarian.

A Ukrainian and another Italian had overtaken Gyurta in the closing stages. Pal's hopes were hanging by a thread, but as time ticked past fifteen minutes, it was clear that he was going to just edge into the final. He qualified in seventh place for the following evening's final.

'At one point, I was thinking how I could go so wrong, coming here with three medal chances to being disqualified in my first race and now this, not being able to make the final of my event. I was really disappointed. I knew it was going to be a good heat, but I just hoped that I would get another chance.'

Pal had watched on intently as the other heats took place. But most of his rivals weren't swimming close to their personal best. 'I was really lucky in the end.'

Talking to his coaches afterwards, Pal tried to ascertain the problems of the heat. Had he pushed it too hard in the first 500 metres? His lactate had peaked too quickly certainly, but if he was to produce a medal-winning swim in the final then he simply had to hope he would feel better.

He tried to recover and the next morning his body felt different, namely that it had 'woken up'. The key for Pal was to take on sugar as soon as his 1500 metres prelim had taken place, to swim down as quickly as possible, take on board a protein drink, a massage and plunge into an ice bath to get the body back to recovery mode. The Danish support team had drummed the importance of the first hour after the race into the squad and then to relax as much as possible – and Pal was adhering to this sage advice.

Before the final, Derk, the MC, was doing a fine job in giving off a Eurovision whiff about proceedings. He was trying to whip the crowd up, asking if certain countries were being represented in the stands. 'Hello, Croatia?' The odd cheer. 'Okaaay, hello… Belarus!' No cheers. And so on.

Given that there was only one Faroese representative in the pool, while support numbered as three – Pal's parents and fiancée, who Pal had proposed to seven months previously in Glasgow following the Duel in the Pool meet – Derk was unlikely to ask for a Faroes cheer.

Pal was nervous come the evening of the final. He was doubting himself, as he did most races. He took some caffeine pills. After his warm up he felt edgy and shaky.

He stood in the call room. He was the second swimmer to walk out. He had the second outside lane, this time there was to be no middle lane as he had experienced in 2010.

'When the gun went off, I just built my frequency of strokes up, working that little bit harder all the time for every 100 or 500 metres. With this game plan, the hope was to maintain a steady pace and by the time the middle 500 metres came, then it was a case of upping the tempo. That's when the racing starts.'

Having covered several 1500 metres races, I had learned to respect the discipline. Before, it was a chance to take stock and write, without any Brits competing, looking up every so often at names you had never heard of. But the 1500 metres had lulled me in.

Certainly you couldn't see the breaking point and endurance of swimmers as much as in, say, the 200m butterfly or the 400m individual medley. Or even, as witnessed in Berlin, in the 4x200m relay when a Swedish swimmer lost five seconds to Italian pin-up Federica Pellegrini on the final leg.

In the 1500 metres there are a range of different tactics. Some go out with one pace in mind, others have an attack point. Pal, meanwhile, is physically built to swim 800 metres all out. He doesn't have to pace himself at that distance, whereas he does at 1500 metres.

If you watch 1500 metres for long enough, it is often a wonder if there are any swimmers who can actually get back from the point where they are overtaken, or look broken. It's very rare to see a swimmer recover their speed and get the lactic out of their muscles.

It wasn't all bad for Pal in the final. He had no one on his inside and he looked to be swimming in the slipstream of Lelliott, the Brit. By 250 metres, Paltrinieri was opening up a very healthy lead and was comfortably inside European record pace.

Back on the Faroes, the national broadcaster was taking a live feed of the race. With Paltrinieri way out in front, it was a nightmare scenario for the commentator ensconced in a booth back in Torshavn. TV pictures were constantly showing the Italian, with little in the way of analysis on Pal.

What I can tell you is this. Detti, who was trying his best to keep with Paltrinieri, was beginning to tire at the 700-metre mark. Before the race, Pal said that Detti might not have too much left in the tank. Or that was his hope at any rate. Lelliott and Pal, swimming side by side, stroke by stroke, were inching closer to Detti and the pair soon overhauled the tanned swimmer from Livorno by the 1000-metre mark.

Lelliott, though, seemed to have the better turn and was also keeping himself in the hunt. Here was the youngest swimmer in the field going toe-to-toe with a European veteran and the oldest of the eight-man field.

At one juncture, Rokur pointed out to me in the press seats that 'Pal's stroke has gone!' Half a lap later, he was forced to eat his words as Lelliott began to feel the pace.

Silver was within Pal's grasp. Detti looked beat, while Lelliott's compatriot, the Scot Stephen Milne, was a couple of seconds down.

Pal went for it. Rokur edged forward in his seats as I tried to keep my press decorum intact by keeping my counsel. All the while, the arena announcer was telling ticket holders inside the velodrome-turned-pool that Paltrinieri was within European record pace, even though the Italian's stroke was by now all over the place. He was hammering his arms down on the water surface just trying to get to the finish.

The record was indeed his – breaking the Russian Yuri Prilukov's 2008 mark – as was his own championship record. Ten seconds later, Pal came home, beating Detti to the wall by a shade under two seconds. From lane 1, Pal had swum one of the cleverest races of his career – not that he had one clue as to where he had actually finished.

'I didn't see Paltrinieri as the Brit was in the way the whole time,' he told me, after conducting interviews in Faroese, Danish and Swedish. 'I was focusing on a progressive swim and as easy a 500-metre swim as possible and from then on doing the best I could. When I passed the British guys, I couldn't see anybody. So I expected at least one Italian out in front. I had to push as much as possible. When I came into second, I was just overjoyed as I had no idea where my other competitors were.'

Listening to Rokur's excitable commentary during the race, it seemed that if Pal was anywhere else apart from lane 1, he might not have won a medal.

'It made me nervous him being in the next door lane. I was afraid he might take me in the last 100 metres but I think we had a really good pace for the first 1000 metres and luckily he had no energy left. After my heat the day before I thought that silver wasn't possible. But I knew I was in shape for this. I felt really bad and I am overjoyed that I got a second chance. I knew there was more in there.'

And my word was he happy when he raised two arms aloft and stepped on to the silver podium later in the evening. There was the swimmers' kindred spirit, too. All three athletes kissed each other on both cheeks before being presented with their medals, while the national anthem was sung with some gusto by the two Italians.

There was traction on social media after the race, too. Twitter was largely still in its infancy in 2010, but this time Pal was getting his fair share of mentions. Not least by a reporter from *The Scotsman*, who joked that with Milne finishing behind Pal it was 'possibly the first instance of Scotland losing to the Faroes at anything (it's been coming)'.

Ah, if only Faroese TV had been here. With such clear water between first and the race for second, the commentator may very well have been caught up in the heat of the moment. Thinking Pal was on for a gallant gold as Detti and Milne were pushed into bronze and fourth respectively, he could have screamed down the mic: 'Mussolini, Ferrari, Berlusconi, Gordon Strachan, Del Amitri… Your boys took one hell of a beating!'

As it was – even if you were Pal's biggest fan (and there are a few of them) – the Faroese media were hardly in the mood to garland one of their own performing on the big stage.

The previous morning, during Pal's preliminary heats, the national radio station was conducting an interview with a well-known Faroese sports journalist on one of his loves: Uruguayan football. After ten minutes his voice became hoarse, so the station then discussed one of the Faroes' former football players, Todi Jonsson, to fill the time. No time, seemingly, to check up on Pal.

The same went for Pal's open water swim, his first on the world stage. This was a chance to add a fresh sub-plot to his career. They create better images, too. However, the front page of the Faroes' national newspaper on that particular morning was a picture of a round table meeting. Nothing political, just Faroese fans of the English Premier League discussing the start of the new season.

We didn't need to ask whether the Faroese media were trumping a possible double medal in the 800 metres. On this occasion, they left it to the German press to deliver. *Die Welt* and another local paper had both interviewed Pal, before Faroese portal site, In.fo, posted the link on their main front page. As Pal's race loomed, the main story was how a village festival had posted a 2,000 krone profit.

At six minutes past six (swimming meets are regimented affairs when it comes to timing), Pal came out last, one arm raised high to acknowledge the sell-out crowd. The loudest reception was most certainly reserved for Paltrinieri, the new kid on the block in European distance swimming who likes to clock up eighteen kilometres per day in training.

Pal had the two Italians – including Detti, the European record holder – on his inside. Whether or not this would hamper him remained to be seen. Considering he only took a breath on his right hand side, Pal would only see the whereabouts of his inside rivals every other fifty metres.

At 300 metres, the young Paltrinieri was a full body length in front. He was going for the European record, without doubt. Pal was holding himself in third in the middle lane; level with Detti and the Czech, Jan Micka.

At halfway, Pal was a smidgen under three seconds down on the nineteen year old, who was flying his way to a double gold. Again, Pal was in the mix for the minor medals. Again, it was intensely close. Who was going to attack? Who was going to break?

Pal's confidence on his entry suggested that he wasn't going to fold. Paltrinieri was slowing down, but the top podium was now his with fifty metres left.

Focus turned to the middle lane and Pal was edging clear of Detti. The medal podium was going to be the same as the 1500 metres. Paltrinieri touched in a championship record 7:44.98, with Pal 3.51 seconds back. Another controlled swim, another silver banked for Pal. It meant that the Faroes had now won two European medals at a major meet for the first time in its history.

It meant another trip down to the media mixed zone. With twenty or so Italian media attempting to gather a sound bite from Paltrinieri, I was again waiting for Pal to emerge as the lone British journalist waiting for a Faroese athlete. This time, I had been joined by Rokur and the man from *Politiken*, the Danish daily.

'It is, it is!' proclaimed Pal when asked whether his two silvers here represented the Faroe Islands' greatest ever championship. 'Two silver medals at the European Championships – that's an improvement by 100 per cent. My mental preparation was totally different to that of the 1500 metres. It could have been a case of saving my championships if I had had a bad race in that final.'

As it was, the prelims of the 800 metres saw several tired swimmers. The Italians were tired, so were the Brits. But beating Detti had given Pal added confidence. Having split the Italians on the podium, he knew the prospects were good for a repeat in that 800 metres.

'Which Italian, I just didn't know! One had the European record in the 800 metres and the other the record in the 1500.'

The mental battle, between Pal and Detti at least, had started with the Faroese's win over his rival in the preliminary swim. He talked to his coaches before the final. The tricky part was not to go all out at the start and not to be afraid of the Italians.

When the gun went off, Detti started at some lick. But Pal felt good. He followed him without taking much out energy-wise over the first 200 metres.

So far so good. It was then that Pal felt the value of being in the moment, perhaps for the first time in his career.

'It was where your thoughts should be, rather than your mind being a helium balloon and going all over the place: what's going to happen, what will happen after this, what medal will it be? Will I even be on the podium? All I thought about was setting up my stroke and keeping my eyes on the other guys. I wasn't thinking about anything else which could ruin my technique.

'I knew my chances were good. If Detti was to beat me then he should have done so over the first half. I beat him in the 1500 metres by overtaking him in the last 300 metres. I had beaten him in the 800 metres prelims in the last 200 metres. So why not do it again here? I believed in myself to do it again. I also believed that Detti had the fear that he couldn't do it. Beating Paltrinieri wasn't an option. Luckily I didn't see him that well and to follow him would have been a suicide mission.

'You have to pick your battles and beating Paltrinieri was only going to happen if he had a bad day. He had a great championship and the focus would be on how to beat him next year. I was so proud how I was able to execute my tactics. How I managed to push through the final 200 metres and see me beat another guy in the finish. That was new to me!'

There was also the thought that Pal could have hauled in Paltrinieri if the race had lasted another fifty metres. 'I heard that he died pretty hard, but swimming alone all the race maybe he didn't feel that good and went out trying to hold it throughout as he does.'

Pal's instinct on turning to look at the scoreboard at the other end of the pool was to hold up two fingers to signify both medals he had won, as well as his two second places.

Pal and Paltrinieri have been Facebook friends way before he became a top swimmer. As a teenager, Paltrinieri was prone to sport some outlandish haircuts, notably a Star Trek-style mop as a teenager.

'That's not how we remember him anymore. That was Paltrinieri being some young Italian kid wanting some recognition when he didn't swim good I guess. It's all change now.'

So a Frenchman, in 2010, now an Italian, in 2014, had thwarted Faroese dreams of gold on the big stage. Two powerful, surging performances leaving the Faroes in second place. Is it ever destined to be? Pal has taken Faroese heroism to a new level, one where the subject is getting stronger, but ultimately falling short of the line. However Pal knows what he said as a ten year old and becoming a world champion was still within his grasp.

'All I need to do now is to cut off five, six, seven seconds – even more in the 1500 – and I don't see that as impossible given my progression.'

Pal's Pool, late 2014

9

PAL'S POOL

A future without Pal is a thought that hasn't quite hit the Faroese yet. In all likelihood, it will be an anti-climax when that day does materialise, with no realistic prospects of ever getting a swimmer to Pal's level again. The Faroese National Championships and Pal's medal haul has proved that.

The Faroese federation sends athletes to compete in many championships and there is plenty of travel, but clubs are under-funded, under-manned and money is spent on a consistent basis. The islands' coaches put pressure on the federation. Parents are doing the same, expressing how swimming in the Faroes should be run.

Such has been Pal's rise that one part of the swimming fraternity believes that the Faroese should be competing at all major championships because the country is now on the sporting map. The reality is that their swimmers are not quite elite status yet, but their times are steadily improving and, if anything, they are beginning to show a healthy work ethic. It is hardly a surprise that two young female swimmers have emerged from Suduroy and have started breaking Faroese senior records in distance swimming. The Pal Effect.

For Faroese swimming, the Island Games have been both a blessing and a curse. Competitors have to qualify just to get there and there is prestige in making the squad for a fairly low standard event. There was huge success in 1989, a 'catastrophe' in 1991, before the age group which saw Pal's emergence won twenty-nine golds at the 2009 Island Games. The Faroese tend to celebrate the Island Games akin to winning a major gold. Pal went for broke on breaststroke, medley, freestyle – and cleaned up.

The modern-day Pal now goes to the Island Games and treats it as a training block, swimming against competitors from twenty-odd islands as diverse as Cayman Islands, Malta, Falkland Islands and Sark.

'I want to push my body, especially mentally, and I want to be able to test my body with events one after the other. Other than that, it's not something I think or get nervous about.'

Pal Joensen competing at the Island Games must represent something of a coup for the organisers. It's like Mark Cavendish turning up at the Island Games and representing the Isle of Man in the cycling events.

Of course, winning the freestyle events would never be a problem for Pal. Now he also uses the Island Games to bag more medals out of his comfort zone, such as the breaststroke and the medley. He calls it 'all good fun' and his last ever Games in 2015 saw him compete with a large-scale Faroese team for the first time since 2011.

His compatriots see him as a leader and the effect he has created throughout Faroese sport meant that he also relished the thought of mentoring the younger squad members as they tasted an international meet in foreign climes.

Pal first raced the biennial Games at Rhodes in 2007. He may be tempted back at the 2021 Island Games, when the Faroes hold the event for the first time since 1989. What's more, the swimming event could even be staged in the Faroes' most southerly island.

**

It was a last-sentence remark in 2010 by Craig Lord, the swimming journalist, which had reignited a bold vision on the island of Suduroy.

'I think that's the first international medal in any sport for my country but in swimming that's a fact,' Pal said on winning European 1500 metres silver in 2010. 'I don't yet know whether I'll stay long-term in the Faroes because the conditions are not very good. I can only train short-course.'

Lord, understanding the complexities of Pal's early training days, signed off his 1500 metres report with: 'Faroe Islands: build that man a 50m pool and name it after him...'

In fact, the first seeds were sown before Budapest, in the months following Pal's three European Junior gold medals. The Faroese Swimming Federation had taken a step back in the project, but Suduroy officials – who oversee a population of under 5,000 – are a stubborn bunch and wanted to deliver a world-class project in harsh conditions, with no involvement from the outside.

'They started out on a three-lane pool, but it flowered into a six-lane project,' said Jon Hestoy. 'It is one of these projects done by sheer willpower alone. Slowly and surely, the building has been completed. It will revolutionise Faroese swimming and will be a fantastic venue for training camps. When we've been out to world meetings, we haven't had a chance in a 50m pool. They've been dead meat. And, because of Pal's success, I can't tell you how many people have said to me "where does this guy of yours train?" They think he is a son of two Faroese people living in southern California, not homebred in a duck pond!'

And so, in 2010, began a remarkable journey in how to build a project on a major scale: a 50m indoor pool to international standard in the furthest island from the capital.

Situated across the fjord and visible from the windows running down the side of the pool at the old swimming club in Vagur, where Pal had learnt his trade, the main building work had yet to start when I visited in 2013.

I was given a tour by Denis Holm, the major of Vagur, the island's town of 1,500 people. He was the brains behind the project, along with his brother.

'Even though he has won three gold medals in the European Juniors and winning titles thereafter, Pal doesn't put himself on a pedestal,' Holm told me as we arced round the fjord to the site. 'He is a normal regular guy, part of a bunch swimming at the pool. You know Mario Balotelli, the footballer? I am Balotelli, I am so great? Pal is so far removed from that. His way of being makes him a great figure for people to look up to. He talks to the young and old and his personality hasn't taken a hit.'

This, along with his success, Holm felt, was the catalyst for the project. 'It was a discussion that Jon Bjarnason, the coach, started due to the talent emerging on Suduroy,' says Holm, two years on. 'Not just Pal but young swimmers who were outgrowing the 12.5m pool they had.'

No one believed in it. Local architects and engineers were shooting the ideas down, mainly due to the project's expense and the complexities involved. Others were bemoaning the idea simply due to the fact that this 50-metre idea was really over one swimmer. Not once did Holm have second thoughts.

Once the silver medal in Budapest had been bagged, Lord had written that one-line comment, and the glorious homecoming from Belgrade to the island had been digested, Holm and four others met. Their naivety, however, suggested that the project might be a step too far.

'It's just about building a house with a big top on it really.'

How difficult can it be?

'But that's where we started. Our attitude was that it really could be possible and we wanted to use local companies and designers to source the materials and give a good price.'

One potential stumbling block was that the pool, of course, had to be exactly fifty metres. It wasn't out of the realms of possibility that a fifty metres and ten centimetres pool could have been created and the Faroes would have become a sporting laughing stock.

So they contacted a dealer in Norway, then an Icelandic outfit, whose technical department travelled over from Italy to the islands to work out the specifications. Once that was cleared, FINA, the world governing body, gave the green light.

Next came the cleaning and the ventilation system. Again, they didn't want to cut corners so they installed the latest model of its kind with expert help. In all, the whole project was made possible thanks to crowdfunding while the sketches were done for virtually nothing thanks to a friend of Holm's.

Then, the team went on a tour of the Faroes to rubber-stamp the project. They visited the Ministry of Culture, who were enthused enough to take it to parliament and look at the possibility of a grant of four million Danish krone (around €500,000).

A 'Pal Loan' was also devised, with the help of a local savings and loans company. The idea was for the implementation of a four-year repayment plan where a fee went to the bank and the rest going into the coffers for the pool. Investors would then be granted free access to the pool and its facilities.

As interest grew and word spread, so islanders raised doubt as to the validity of the project. One Member of Parliament wrote an open letter to the public in the local newspaper, saying it was more or less 'a bogus project'. Jon Hestoy, the then-Faroese Swimming president, wrote in response for the politician to give some fact to his argument or otherwise support the project.

'To them we were some local lunatics who didn't know anything about building a pool,' says Holm. 'For our vision was to complete the project for two million euros. To the professionals, the designers, engineers and architects – they thought it impossible: eight million-plus euros was a more likely figure. But our final cost calculations were set on two million and parliament found it difficult to accept. So we flipped it over. We said, "You can give us four million krone, but you don't have to pay it unless we finish the building."'

Their tour continued, with Pal travelling alongside Holm. Companies were positive. They were excited about the project and wanted to invest. 'We asked them whether they wanted publicity, but they turned it down and simply said that we had a vision that few others had.'

The crowdfunding project saw backing from large companies and municipalities and Holm was obliged, through their backers and the Faroese parliament, to bid out to professional companies for the main construction work.

One company came back with a €300,000 cost. 'A crazy price,' thought Holm. So he contacted another engineering firm, who told him that the figure was conceived purely because the project was going to be outside of the capital, Torshavn. In the end, a €50,000 figure was settled on.

The crowdsourcing initiative then saw Holm seek expert knowledge, without payment. With this help the whole building saw further cuts in the total costs.

So, when a specific question on lighting was needed, a local expert came in and said he would do it for free. Free workforce is hardly commonplace these days, but Suduroy had it in spades. Call it community spirit.

Or was it the climate and Suduroy's distance from the capital that spurred the mayor and his vision? Holm believes the climate forces the islanders to have more social contact. If there is a special project to be done, they all work together.

Holm continued to reach out to the community. He sent out a message on Facebook looking for skilled workers to install heating on the floors; the next day fifteen islanders turned up and they completed the job for free. The same applied to the insulation and paint work. 'We haven't paid one euro in salaries, which is a fantastic thing for us to say.'

As luck would have it, the positioning of the pool was also going to play a pivotal part in the project's future. Why are there so few pools in the Faroes (the last one was built in 1984)? For one, the heating costs so much, as oil is used.

But the Pal Pool was going to use surplus heat from the power plant, located just fifty metres from the site. Besides the building cost, the main expense comes from heating the water, so without the power plant the project's monthly bills would have made for gloomy reading.

In this day and age of declining sports facilities, especially in the UK, where councils are caving in to flat-hungry developers, the Pal Pool is a refreshing antidote.

'This community has a history of doing big things on a voluntary basis. We have a portal for just this. So, for example, if there is a project that needs doing, they put it out looking for volunteers.'

The same applied for the Pal Pool where they were looking for volunteers one Saturday morning. Feel free to come, they had said. It wasn't just a trickle: thirty-five turned up and they were able to complete another tick on Holm's to-do list, all inside just two hours. Again, they didn't pay a single Danish krone for the work.

They were also able to complete insulation on the building thanks to Suduroy manpower. Fifteen arrived one Monday morning, a working day, and it was completed inside four hours.

Holm believes that the reason why the pool has worked out so cheap is that they have questioned every facet of the project that has cost the most. They then locked heads and figured a way of making it cheaper.

For example, the engineer employed to do the ventilation system was asked for a calculation on how much it would cost in the real marketplace. Well, he said, it would probably cost close to €250,000. They were then fixed on trying to do it for €100,000. They ended up spending not a euro more once it was finished.

As word spread of the project – Holm says that it was known throughout the Nordic regions – so did negotiations on price. A Danish dealer found himself talking to an Icelandic swimming pool company one day, who gave a 'super price' on painting the inside of the pool. Holm admitted that it cost twice the price of painting the inside of his own house.

On went the work, the free or cut-price services. The Icelandic company responsible for the roof and windows had heard of Pal's rise and this unique project. They cut thirty per cent off the retail price.

Nearly five years on from their first meeting stands a six-lane 50m pool, a children's pool, fitness and wellness centre.

Once word had travelled across the Norwegian Sea, Holm began to be contacted. The costs of building pools in Denmark are equally high and soon representatives were eager to know how on earth a 50m one could be built on the Faroes' most southerly island.

In the end Team Denmark, the country's Olympic body, got in touch. In a book detailing Team Denmark's last thirty years, three pages were devoted to the Pal project, suggesting that Danes should travel to the Faroes and wonder how a small community can build a pool of this calibre in such harsh environs. If the Faroes can, so could Denmark.

However, one wonders how much impact the pool will have on the community. Judging by the emails Holm received even before completion and publicity, he had five requests from national teams wanting to come and train at the facility over a ten-day or so period.

On the back of this, a meeting was held and it was decided that eight summer houses should be built with eighty beds.

In all, Holm, together with his brother, Jon, encountered no stumbling blocks during the project, or indeed any budget struggles. There were no time constraints. The only obstacle came from the dissenters.

There was the lip service, says Holm, from positive Faroese. Then, when building work did commence, came the rumours from the capital; those who thought it wasn't possible. 'That wasn't so funny,' he admits. 'But I think we had a bit of balls.'

What Holm means is that the project took on the mantle of a poker game. 'We had a handful of aces, but really we didn't at all!'

But, in the early throes of the project, once they had borrowed the machinery to clear the ground for the initial paving of cement and the laying of the first foundations, only then did islanders and beyond sit up and the money started to come in.

Every Sunday, the Holms held a 'building meeting', either to talk about what needs doing or going to the site and discussing the next phase of Pal's Pool and the Faroe Islands Aquatic Centre.

'Pal may not have been a part of the project, despite him travelling to the meetings to secure sponsorship, but he is still the icon. Whole communities can live on something like this and building something crazy as a 50m pool for a community of only 1,350. How crazy is that!'

Pal was living on Suduroy when plans were first mooted. Midway through the project, he moved to Copenhagen with his fiancée, but he still travelled to sponsorship meetings when he could. When he returns to open the centre, it will be in his name.

'It is truly an amazing feat, very cool to see and I am very proud to have a pool named after me. Not only for a small town in the Faroe Islands, but a symbol of optimism and hard work has that got results. I just don't think you can do something like this elsewhere and projects like this only works in small communities such as Suduroy. I don't know from experience, but as soon as a project gets big and goes over budget, more commonly than not it fails.

'It is a dream from a small plan. A lot of people were questioning whether it is sustainable, but the amazing thing is that a collective community has stood together and built something that no one else in the world has been able to achieve, especially in such a small place! To get an energy company to let them run the heating into the pool – I don't think you will ever get that!'

As the building developed and nurtured, so coach Bjarnason would look out of the Susvim pool windows on the other side of the fjord and think to himself 'oh, one day I won't have to walk back and forth down the 25m pool deck'. From 12.5m to 25m to 50m, Jon could finally put his plans into place after being restricted for so many years.

'We just didn't have the space, the equipment or anything. Those restrictions are gone and the sky's the limit. We have built a name for ourselves and people know we have existed because of the "effect" of Pal. We have bookings into the future from Norway and Denmark. There are swim teams from Germany who are excited about the place. They know about Pal's physique and conditioning and they want to know if success really is down to genetics, what we do in training here or if it's what Pal has eaten. They know about Pal's long endurance tests on treadmills and they are off the charts. The experienced coaches want to find out more. It's exciting.'

Suduroy will also surely hold the first Faroese Long Course Championships in the not too distant future. Commonly, 50-metre events are held in Iceland in January. 'It's not the best of times,' laughs Jon. 'We have twenty-one hours of darkness in that time. Everyone is chronically tired and sleepy. Nobody is swimming fast in January, so I'm looking forward to having a midsummer's Long Course Championships for sure.'

No one, not even a visionary coach such as Jon could have imagined this. Not even when the pair were on the back of the open truck after Belgrade 2008.

Then, on islands where most sons follow their father's career, Suduroy had celebrated a homecoming from Serbia which might have well have had a sociological impact on its future.

Ever since coach Bjarnason could remember, Suduroy had been slowly 'dying' in population. In the eighties, he remembers his school with 500 pupils, with numbers slowly decreasing to around 200.

Pal's success, says Jon, is now being transcended across the islands, used in every aspect of society. 'He is being used the whole time as an example and I truly believe his success has helped the population in this regard.'

Pal may be used to the growing accolades he has accumulated as an elite swimmer, but not even this affable Faroese could even begin to contemplate how the project would turn out once the doors were swung open for the first time.

'I can't imagine how it's going to be. For me, it's like a chemical reaction. I've just done what I love to do and perhaps I think as myself as the spark to the flame for what the people have been able to achieve – and not much more than that. I don't think as myself as the builder of the pool, but the reason. Some ask why they built the pool when I'm never going to train in it. But that was never the purpose of the pool. It was never to get me to return and train there. Reality was going to tell us that that was never going to happen.

'It's a way of getting new activities in the community which were otherwise fading out. Denis has really revived the islands and he has certainly got the potential out of Vagur and the surrounding areas of what can be achieved. And this was a major way to do it. In essence, it is a symbol to tell people of what can be achieved. People tell me that I am an ambassador, thanks to my swimming, that I have achieved what nobody else has done on the island. I think the swimming pool is a symbol of that too.'

Copenhagen is closer to London than it is to Suduroy, but Pal's Pool can also be a symbol for the next generation of swimmer to emerge from the Faroes, with the nation's number 1 sportsman residing in a different country – and having to swim for his adopted country at the Olympics.

'They built the pool because of what he was doing,' says Thurid, Pal's mother. 'They always knew that Pal would not stay on the island. To be educated you have to leave the island. So the pool is not to him but he is the reason why. People are proud of Pal here. They are proud that the pool has been built.'

Compared to how it felt before, just Pal and Jon going to events, he never had a feel that he was part of an international team, part of a swimming nation with all the perks that sit alongside it. Starting to train with the Danes changed his conceptions, though it has taken five years for it to be cemented.

'Always in the back of my head, there was the thought that I was going to swim for Denmark. It never occurred to me that this would be the case. Being part of a team is only a good thing, people say. But when you aren't used to it, I don't really agree. I wouldn't put that much emphasis on it, but it certainly was a different feeling.'

Today, Pal is always included in meetings. He travels with the team and feels a strong sense of unity towards those famous red outfits.

He's inexorably risen from a weak athlete into a world-class swimmer. He's no laughing stock either. He's still only a small fish in the world of swimming and on a wider sporting context, when compared to the likes of Michael Phelps and Katie Ledecky at least.

However, Pal has given the Faroe Islands a reason to believe. They'll continue to support him and will continue to cheer him on, even when he's swimming for Denmark.

But he will always be Faroese.

'Farewell!' Faroes
Here in this strange, forgotten land
Lie things my heart alone could tell,
Some lure or mystery perchance
In silvery sea and barren fell.
People strange of dress, they seem
A vision of a bygone year;
On waistcoats red the buttons gleam
Like sunshine on a falling tear.
An island bleak and swept with rain;
The skies go grey with winter's snow;
The cliffs I shall not see again
Stand proud behind me as I go.
My thoughts on greater islands dwell,
Across the waves, where sky meets sea.
To Faroe Isles I say 'Farewell!'
And greet the land still home to me.

From *Fanfaroe*, British Armed Forces publication, 1943.

TACKLING THE 1500 METRES
Rod Gilmour

My quest to experience a 1500 metres swim in a Sussex pool similar to Pal's early days hit murky waters from the outset.

'A 12.5m pool!?' Pal messaged me. 'Well, there are going to be a lot of turns and you're going to get dizzy. I think you could start at a pace where you don't get too dizzy and when you get used to it you can work yourself into a nice groove. But I gotta say, it does not sound pleasant.'

I then posted a message on Facebook, asking for advice on technique and what I should eat beforehand. 'You definitely need some dried fish, whale meat and whale blubber,' was the only response I had back.

It was a pertinent comment. I hadn't mentioned whales once in *The Pal Effect* and here I was being reminded as the project ended.

For those unaware, the Faroe Islands' mystical beauty is hampered by an annual controversy over what locals call the *Grindadráp*, a Faroese whale slaughter. When whales are spotted close to the islands during this *Grindadráp*, or grind, fishermen drop what they're doing and soon a flotilla of small vessels is out at sea. The aim is to create an arc and drive the animals into a shallow bay where waiting locals can use their ancient knives to kill the whales.

Animal rights activists have been trying to stop these grinds since the eighties. The images that are sent out by its detractors, one of blood-filled waters, hardly paint an idyllic picture of the islands. But many locals defend the killings as a cultural right, the Faroes having had to defend itself from the elements over the centuries, not least from starvation. Moreover, the whale meat is not sold for commercial use, only cut and shared between the islanders.

Whatever opinion is formed, the fact remains that as the seas get more polluted, so the level of mercury and other toxins heightens. It means that whale meat consumption has reduced somewhat and is ill-advised to eat. Hence, I was unlikely to rush out for the meat ahead of my 1500 metres tilt.

All in all, a less than auspicious start, but I had two positives on my side: I was never going to find a suitable 12.5m pool in my county, while the thought of doing sixty flip turns was definitely off the agenda.

One early spring morning, I drove the five minutes from my house to the 25m local community pool in Ringmer, East Sussex. All well and good so far, I was replicating Pal, although I certainly didn't have to take the bus to Brighton as he would have done in his early days in Copenhagen.

I then discovered that, due to a staff shortage, the pool was shut. A mad dash back home ensued, arriving just in time to take my two daughters off my wife's hands and to school. She was only too glad to accept.

My daughters' school pool is a venue I am able to swim at twice a week after drop-off. On Tuesdays, I am the only male swimmer, alongside six or so mothers, and I managed to find a lane at the side to see through my quest.

With no drills or technique banked, nor intervals, speed work or endurance sessions for that matter, I had coach Bjarnason's words ringing in my ears after Skyping Suduroy's top coach the previous day.

'Start out slow. In fact, start out as if you are going too slow. Get a breathing rhythm from the very beginning and start breathing right away. Don't think too much about technique as it will stress your shoulders and you will tire easily. Swimmers like to spread their knees too much when they kick. Keep your legs together and the only thing to think about is to keep them up horizontally.'

For the first 250 metres, I imagined the sight of the bald-headed Jon, in his Susvim tracksuit, barking orders at me as I contemplated sixty lengths of front crawl when my twice-weekly ritual consisted of one length crawl, one length breaststroke. It was just easier and more comfortable.

After 100 metres I decided to try different tactics and started doing six strokes breathing to the right. In races, I had seen Pal only breathe on his right and Jon had explained that this was purely down to habit. His motor skills 'were one of the poorest' he had seen 'of anyone' when Pal had first started out, who had also found it difficult to change anything in those first early throes in the pool.

As the pair forged their relationship, Pal kept to breathing on his right in his races, but made sure he evened it out in training by breathing on his left, lessening the stress on his shoulders.

I remember Jon describing Pal's arms as, 'amongst the strongest in the world. I've never seen anyone beat him for front crawl pull.' Thirty lengths in to my sixty-length effort, I wished to have Pal's arms. It felt like I was swimming against the tide.

The reason I find swimming so beneficial is when that moment arrives where everything clicks. It usually comes after fifteen minutes or so. The muscles are relaxed, a rhythm is found and all is good with the world. I find that some of my best ideas for a day's work ahead come in that period, not having to worry about anything else.

Liam Tancock, the Exeter backstroker, may have been referring to his tapering when he told me that 'the change in feeling is phenomenal and it makes all the difference' in hitting the water, but the same could be applied to the feeling I get after that initial ten to fifteen minutes in the water.

At some point after the 750-metre mark, I realised that I wasn't going to beat the time of the first known world record, that of Britain's Henry Taylor at the 1908 Olympics in London, who swam 22:48.4. In fact I was going to be trumped too by the Rwandan swimmer Jackson Niyomugabo, who had bravely plodded on at the 25m World Championships in 2010, posting over twenty-three minutes and finishing some six minutes after the last swimmer had finished.

As the pool of mothers began to empty, so did my energy. The last ten lengths were uneventful, the picture of Australian Ian Thorpe in the pool reception spurring me on in those final lengths. My time? A leisurely 41:23. I'll stick to my front crawl-breaststroke next time.

It was, though, a prior conversation I'd had with one mother, Jax, which lingered afterwards. As we had goggled up, she'd mentioned a BBC Radio 4 programme that she had heard a few months previously, admitting that the short, five-minute feature had changed the way she had approached her swimming.

I searched for the programme and came across a BBC listening project called 'Paddy and Mick, Swimming and Philosophy'. The story centred on two softly-spoken Ulstermen who had met through meditation but also had a penchant for swimming in the wild waters of Northern Ireland.

I listened in to their conversation and it is the final minute which resonated.

Mick: As well as the meditative side of swimming, there is the philosophical side too: what is the best way to swim to A to B? Is it to take a stroke and your hand is open in the water? And you learn that you have much better purchase on the water if your hand is open, than if you try and grab a handful of water with your fist.

Paddy: In our lives, things come and go and we can make life a lot more difficult by trying to hang on to things that are leaving us. After a swim everything seems alright with the world even if you have to go back to the humdrum of life and go back to do the groceries. It's that freshness, you have that appetite sharpened and sometimes you can follow it with chips.

Mick: I think, definitely, a swim is complete if it ends with chips. [They both laugh.]

PAL IS A LIVING, BREATHING FAROESE HERO

Rokur i Jakupsstovu,
President of the Faroe Islands Swimming Federation

Being in the pool always feels like summer for me. It means a lot when you come from a place like the Faroe Islands, a country that has autumn weather, with wind and rain, pretty much all year round. It is blissful to dive into the hot waters and be weightless for a while.

Through all of this, through the rise of Pal, one of my favourite things to do is to go down to our little seventies-style, brown-tiled pool and swim alone with a few of the regulars.

I have made it into my own little tradition to do, every once in a while, at least 1500 metres in homage to our living legend Pal Joensen – and preferably about 2000 metres, to be able to keep up with the masters' swimmers of the Nordic Federation, when we meet for conferences and mandatory morning swims.

It is a kind of meditation, switching between strokes but seldom stopping. I try to keep count but I don't really care if I lose it. It is way more 'Zen' than any combat sport I've tried.

My earliest swimming memory is from a beach near Copenhagen, when my parents studied there in the seventies. I remember my father standing leg-deep and trying to teach me how to swim. 'Because I don't,' he had said.

I remember an old open air pool in Torshavn where we had swim classes at school. I remember understanding why the sauna had been installed: well, we used it for heating ourselves up between stints in the cold water. I remember debris like leaves and dead insects and a live daddy longlegs that I was afraid of.

As a teenager, I remember swimmers of the same age as me looking like Greek gods, with their six-packs and muscled arms. For good reasons, I tried other sports. Never a good footballer, I ended up first in judo, and later taekwondo.

I went on a one-year high school exchange programme when I was about seventeen to the Shetland Islands, where Ove Joensen had rowed to.

I had put on too much weight by then and was uncomfortable about that. To be frank, I was also quite struck by claustrophobia with the Shetland Isles' capital, Lerwick, being even smaller than Torshavn.

My room-mate got me into vegetarianism, which, coupled with our landlord demanding us to shut off the electrical heating at night, meant we experienced some really cold nights. One guy came up with the brilliant idea of taking brisk walks late in the evening, so that we would be warmed up before going to bed.

That developed into running for my part when I returned prematurely to the Faroe Islands. I had too much time on my hands and stumbled upon this new sport called triathlon. So I started doing that, first with a basic bike and later with one that I bought second hand from a participant at the 1989 Island Games.

I swam beside the lane ropes of the Torshavn swim club, HS, so as not to have to meddle too much with the old ladies. Then one day while standing at the window at the entrance, the head coach came over to me and asked if I would like to join the club.

Study and life soon took over though. I became a father while still at school, and ended up returning from Denmark and moving in with my wife, Lis, in her hometown of Toftir.

Then, one day, she told me that a woman had mentioned to her at the local grocery store whether I was in a position to take a head coach role for the local swim club, FLOT.

I was flattered and accepted the unpaid job, wondering how on earth they had heard about me. It turned out later that it was my swim mate from Torshavn, who had taught me breaststroke and was now head coach in Klaksvík. The club was desperate for a coach.

I had to deal with swimmers leaving after about the third year into the job. On top of dealing with this, I was working, commuting and coaching. I was feeling burnt out.

In 1999, the swim federation asked me to go with two swimmers to the 1999 European Junior Championships in Moscow. It was a really desperate situation, as they had just said goodbye to the national coach and had suffered a miserable Island Games in Gotland.

The following year, the federation gathered most of us for a planning weekend in Vagar, led by Flemming Poulsen, the former national coach of Denmark. The federation was in a bit of a crisis, having trouble finding medals at the Island Games after a good stint in the nineties. I remember proclaiming that we wanted to medal at international meets in maybe ten years, but I didn't really believe it.

At the end of the weekend, the then president of the federation asked me if I would like to go to Aalborg in Denmark to study to become an elite coach, with financial support from the federation. The school started the following in a week, or thereabout.

My mother was in Copenhagen, receiving treatment for cancer. I talked to my wife, and ended up signing up, leaving her back home with our two daughters. It still haunts me that she cried when I left our car for the air shuttle bus in Torshavn.

Coaching school was very beneficial. I learned a lot on the practical side and being assistant coach to Jon Bjarnason, who was over there at the time. My mother got well again, too.

I had wanted to find a coaching job in Denmark, but chose the easy path and ended up as head coach of the swim club in Torshavn. I enjoyed the experience of a busy role, until I was fired after a row at a swim meet in late 2002.

My team had wanted to leave in protest over the referee, and I had let them. I was quarantined by the federation for three months and ended up winning the appeal. Being fired with no warning was a serious wake-up call and it made me give up on the dream of being a full-time coach.

After a year as an accountant, I ended up as an IT consultant. I was also approached by the federation, asking if I could be their commentator in the TV broadcast for the Faroese National Championships, a role I still revel in.

In 2007, I did what I believe is the one bad call of my blogging career – I also have a swim website, svimjing.com – when I proclaimed that it was a waste of money to send our first team to the World Championships in Melbourne that spring, including Pal. They ended up doing okay and Pal decided to aim even higher.

Life started getting really interesting with Pal's emergence and Belgrade 2008 was a week-long celebration and laughing ourselves silly.

A year later I ended up as vice-president of the Faroe Islands Swimming Federation, and in 2014 I became the president. Both of these positions have meant a whole lot more work and responsibilities, but also opportunities that have led me to all the major meets that Pal has been to since Belgrade, except the London 2012 Olympics.

It has been a rollercoaster ride, but it feels like it is just speeding up, with us hanging on as well as we can. I like to compare Faroese swimming with swans or synchro swimmers: it might look graceful on top, but we work for dear life below the water line.

And with Pal and Faroese swimming in general, it turns out that we are actually quite good at it. You could say we were 'born to do this', a people of coastal fishermen who for centuries had to row long and hard in order not to starve so much in the winter. Only the most stubborn stayed, rather than leave for greener pastures. There, you have the Faroe spirit.

For centuries we were the 'small guy', not really believing in ourselves when our bigger neighbours and invaders told us the lay of the land. In sport, we always talked about 'honourable losses', but then Pal came along and showed us that it only takes one determined guy to make big waves. And little by little, we all started to realise that there might be strength in being so few.

Faroese swimming is extremely fragile though, with the majority of the Faroese and, most importantly, the Faroese mainstream media still sticking to football. I am not sure whether we will be able to keep the steam up, or crumble and fall back to the situation we were once in.

It won't keep us from having fun while it lasts. We have had the opening of Pal's pool in Vagur and have ongoing projects, like spearheading a better lifeguarding system in public pools and schools, and getting our own swim education into place. We're also working with universities to hopefully make a better physical testing protocol for swimmers.

I myself couldn't be happier. It is a gift having Pal. I've been very privileged to follow him throughout his career. I have an excellent wife who knows that I have spent many days of my holiday for this. My kids love it, too. They have a father who rides with Pal Joensen.

Either Pal is the only one or he is the first. He is either the one or only sports hero on the Faroe Islands at international level, or he is the first. He will never be second to anything.

It is also a question of what I can tell my grandchildren in future years. Whether there once was this Faroese swimmer, or whether there will be future athletes who can follow in his footsteps.

For now, he is the living, breathing sports hero of the Faroe Islands.

We few, we happy few.

WE DON'T TEND TO BRAG IN THE FAROES

Malan Joensen, wife of Pal Joensen

Growing up on Suduroy was every child's dream. A paradise where nature rules, where everybody knows everybody, where there is no crime, where one doesn't need to lock the door when leaving home and where all your friends and family are always close. It has got to be the most beautiful and peaceful place on earth.

Living the island life is a slow-paced life, where 'if we don't make it today, there's always tomorrow' rules. Growing up, there wasn't that much to do besides playing sports; no cinema, shopping centre, restaurants, cafés and so on, but this is exactly what makes it so special. I myself chose swimming as a hobby, and that's where I first met Pal.

It soon became clear to me, that here was a young athlete who did not intend to live in the belief that he couldn't achieve his dreams.

When I was fifteen years old and I started dating Pal I quickly found out that he was a young man with strong dreams. One who saw opportunities where everyone else saw problems and obstacles.

Already in 2007, after the Nordic Junior Championships held in the Faroe Islands in December, and where Pal won three gold medals, it was clear that he was ready to do what it takes to reach the top.

'Yes,' he said bluntly, 'I'm going to be world champion one day.' There is no doubt that there have been people around the islands shaking their heads and thinking that this was a cute childhood dream. For us who knew Pal there was no doubt to it – he meant every word!

The dream that began to sprout in Pal's mind required much hard work to be realised, but he was aware of that and he was willing to do whatever it took.

Preparations for the European Junior Championships in Belgrade in July 2008 began. Jon Bjarnason had come to coach our swimming club a few years earlier and he totally changed our training mentality.

We learned that it takes hard work to reach the top, but also that hard work eventually pays off. In late July it was time for Pal to shine on the international swimming stage for the first time. And he did what none of us had thought possible he would do, not in our wild imaginations at least. He became European Junior champion – three times!

We knew that Pal was well prepared for these championships, but I would lie if I said we expected him to become a triple champion. He honestly took us all by surprise, including himself.

His family and I, who were all with him in Belgrade, had spent the last couple of days in Serbia ecstatic and overly happy, but Pal himself, calm as usual, did not seem to realise just how big his achievements were and what a big deal this was.

We don't tend to brag and put ourselves on a pedestal. Pal, who has largely trained in a small pool, looked at the obstacles and said, okay, I can do this anyhow. That has always been his strength.

On our way back home to the Faroe Islands again, it became clear that the entire country was ready to celebrate Pal's victories. After landing in Vagar Airport, the red carpet was rolled out and fire trucks stood spraying water on the plane.

A day of celebration had begun, one that included many interviews, flowers, speeches and even an afternoon tea with the Prime Minister, before leaving on the ferry for Suduroy. The celebration continued on the ferry, but for Pal it still hadn't sunk in.

As the ferry docked, we were told to go outside and watch the giant crowds of people who were there to celebrate Pal's victory. That's when he realised what he'd done.

It's a moment I will never forget, watching hundreds of people waving flags and shooting fireworks – and all of a sudden Pal looked at me, truly amazed, and burst into tears. He was totally overwhelmed.

We were taken by an open truck to Pal's hometown of Vagur, where even more people were waiting for him to arrive. This was a very emotional day and one I will never forget – but this was just the beginning!

Now it was time to set and chase the next goal, and the Olympics in London 2012 became the main goal. On his road to London there were both ups and downs, as it took time trying to reach the senior elite.

In August 2010, Pal took silver in the 1500 metres freestyle at the European Championships in Budapest and he had now officially joined the elite. In July 2011 he took fourth place in the 1500 metres at the World Long Course Championships in Shanghai, and he was now more ready than ever for the Olympics.

But there was this one thing; if he wanted to go to the Olympics, he was going to have to switch his Faroes cap with a Danish one.

This was something that made some Faroese people upset, but for Pal there was no doubt in his heart – if the alternative was not going to the Olympics, he was going to have to live with upsetting some people and just keep the Faroese flag in his heart while competing under the Danish one. The road to London was fun and tough, but it was all going be worth it in the end. As we now know, this was sadly not the case. Life had to go on, and this included moving to Denmark, starting a new chapter in life.

We began studying, and Pal became part of the Danish team at the National Training Centre in Copenhagen. This meant new focus points at training and Pal was soon a well-integrated part of the team. We love this stage in life and living in Copenhagen.

Almost all of our Faroese friends from back home also live and study here, so sometimes we tend to even forget we live in another country.

We do not know what the future holds for us, but moving back home has always been a part of the plan for the future. Until then, we enjoy life here in Copenhagen and hold the Faroe Islands close to our heart.

RECORDS AND MEDALS
(as of May 2015)
Statistics supplied by Bartal Hojgaard

800m freestyle, long course: 7:45.55, 2011 Shanghai (World Championships)

800m freestyle, short course: 7:36.24, 2011 Atlanta (Duel In The Pool)

1500m freestyle, long course: 14:46.33, 2011 Shanghai (World Championships)

1500m freestyle, short course: 14:26.54, 2011 Dubai (World Championships)

At the 2007 Faroese National Championships, the first time Pal had swum the 1500m, he posted a time of 17:08.81.

Pal has held the Faroese record in the 1500m short course since 2006 when he first took the record with a time of 16:03.59. The record at the time was 16:27.93 by Bogi Lemvig set in 1999.

On January 17, 2007 Pal was the first Faroese to go under sixteen minutes in the 1500m. He clocked 15:56.21 at a competition in his hometown, Vagur.

Former president of the Faroese Swimming Association, Jon Hestoy, was close to becoming the first Faroese swimmer to go under sixteen minutes when, in 1982 at the Danish Short Course Championships, he swam 16:00.09. However, it was never an official Faroese record. The second Faroese to go under sixteen minutes was Oli Mortensen, in 2012, with 15:53.39.

The third Faroese to break the sixteen-minute mark was Alvi Hjelm in 2012, with 15:48.58. Marius Ihlen Gardshodn swam 15:49.42 in April 2015.

Since Faroese swimming records began over forty years ago, there have never been more than one or two long-distance swimmers at any time. Seeing three swimmers break through the sixteen-minute mark in recent years is an example of the Pal effect in action.

Pal was the first Faroese swimmer to achieve 900 FINA ranking points or more, achieving the mark in July 2008 (902 points) on long course 1500m freestyle, with his time of 15:20.13.

Pal was also, with this time, the first Faroese under sixteen minutes over 1500m. This was posted just two weeks before his triumphant winning time (15:18.37) in Belgrade at the 2008 European Junior Championships.

His 2010 European silver winning time in Budapest (also a Nordic record) was his first long course time under fifteen minutes (14:56.90).

Pal earned his golden pin (a Faroese mark for achieving 730 FINA points and a symbol of elite status across genders and discipline) in the 400m freestyle in November 2006. He was the seventeenth swimmer to reach the mark. As of May 2015, thirty-nine swimmers have won the golden pin – again an example of 'The Pal Effect' in motion.

Pal was the first to get the Faroese golden pin, with 864 FINA points at the 2010 National Championships. This new honorary pin was introduced the week before, inadvertently due to the new golden era of Faroese swimming.

In late September 2010, Pal was at Team Denmark's test centre where he set the best physical scores (muscle strength and max VO2) of any swimmer, including Lotte Friis, Mads Glæsner and Aschwin Wildeboer.

In February 2012, Pal set an unofficial 5000m and 3000m long course Danish record at altitude training camp in South Africa. His record breaking time at 5000m was 50:00.18.

At the 2013 Faroese National Championships, Pal won his hundredth medal. A year later he won his hundredth gold medal on 17 May – and the next day his hundredth individual gold medal.

2007

Gold in 400m and 1500m freestyle in Reykjavík International, bronze in 200m freestyle

Five gold medals and 1 bronze at NatWest Island Games on Rhodes (gold in 200m, 400m and 1500m freestyle, 4x50m freestyle, 4x50m medley. Bronze in 4x100m medley)

2008

Gold in 400m, 800m and 1500m freestyle at Beograd (European Juniors)

Silver in 1500m freestyle at World Cup in Stockholm. 4th in 400 m free

5th place in 1500m in European Short Course championships in Rijeka, Croatia

2009

Gold in 200m, 400m and 1500m free and 200m backstroke in Reykjavík International, bronze in 200m butterfly and 200m medley

Bronze in 400 free in Paris Open. 4th in 1500m

8 gold, 6 silver and 2 bronze at NatWest Island Games in Aland, Sweden (gold in 50m, 100m, 200m, 400m and 1500m free - a first in the Games - gold in 200m breaststroke and 50m butterfly, gold in 4x50m medley, silver in 100m, 200m and 400m medley, silver in 4x100m freestyle and 4x100m medley, silver in 50 breaststroke, bronze in 100 breaststroke and 200m butterfly)

Gold in 1500m World Cup in Moscow and silver in Berlin

Finals in 400m and 1500m freestyle in European Short Course Championships in Istanbul

2010

Gold in 800m freestyle in South African Championships and bronze in 1500m

5th in 400m freestyle at Mare Nostrum, Monaco

Bronze in 1500m at Mare Nostrum, Canet. 5th in 400m freestyle

Silver in 1500m freestyle at European Long Course Championships in Budapest

Silver in 400m and 1500m freestyle at World Cup in Berlin

Gold in 400m and 1500m at World Cup in Moscow

Silver in 1500m freestyle and bronze in 400m freestyle in World Cup, Stockholm

Finals in World Short Course Championships in Dubai

2011

Gold in 200m and 400m freestyle in Bergen Swim Festival, Norway

8 gold, 4 silver and 1 bronze at NatWest Island Games on Isle of Wight (gold in 100, 200, 400 and 1500m freestyle, 200m breaststroke and 400m medley, and in 4x50m and 4x100m freestyle

Silver in 100m and 200m medley. Bronze in 100m breaststroke)

Finals in 800m and 1500m freestyle at World Championships in Shanghai (fifth and fourth, respectively)

Gold in 1500m freestyle at World Cup, Stockholm and bronze in 400m freestyle

4th in 400m and 1500m freestyle at European Championships in Stettin

Gold in 800m freestyle at Duel in the Pool in Atlanta, with fourth fastest time ever

2012

London 2012 Olympics: 400m and 1500m freestyle (tenth in 400m)

10th in the 5K European Open Water Championships in Piombino

5th in 400m freestyle at World Cup, Berlin. Finals of 1500m

Bronze in 1500m freestyle at World Short Course Championships in Istanbul. 6th in 400m freestyle

2013

Gold in 400m and 1500m freestyle at Flanders Speedo Cup 2013

Gold in 400m freestyle, silver in 200 freestyle at Bergen Swim Festival

4th in 400m freestyle at Mare Nostrum, Barcelona

4th in 1500m freestyle at Mare Nostrum, Canet. 7th in 400m freestyle

Finals of World Long Course Championships in Barcelona (seventh in 800m and 1500m freestyle)

Silver in 1500m freestyle at European Short Course Championships in Herning, Denmark

Silver in 800m freestyle at the Duel in the Pool, Glasgow

2014

Gold in 1500m freestyle at Swim Cup Eindhoven

Gold in 400m freestyle, bronze in 200m freestyle at Bergen Swim Festival

Silver in 400m freestyle at Mare Nostrum in Monaco

Silver in 1500m freestyle at Mare Nostrum in Ba

Silver in 800m and 1500m freestyle at European long course Championships

ACKNOWLEDGEMENTS

To Rokur i Jakupsstovu and Jon Hestoy, for not only the wealth of information you supplied me and background into Faroese swimming, but also your kind hospitality over the last five years. Without your help, this would not have been possible. To Bartal Hojgaard, Rokur's brother, for statistics and records. To Visit Faroes for travel and Mika at Travel PR for backing the project, Scott Reeves at Chequered Flag Publishing and, of course, Pal and Malan, for believing in the book from our first meeting.

INNOVATIVE AND EXCITING SPORTS BOOKS

www.chequeredflagpublishing.co.uk